Mammissima

Mammissima

Family cooking from a modern Italian mamma

Elisabetta Minervini

BLOOMSBURY
LONDON · OXFORD · NEW YORK · NEW DELHI · SYDNEY

For Eleonora and Emiliano

Bloomsbury Publishing
An imprint of Bloomsbury Publishing Plc
50 Bedford Square, London, WC1B 3DP, UK
1385 Broadway, New York, NY 10018, USA

www.bloomsbury.com

BLOOMSBURY and the Diana logo are trademarks of Bloomsbury Publishing Plc

First published in Great Britain 2016
Text © Elisabetta Minervini, 2016
Photography © Jonathan Kennedy, 2016
Illustrations © Babeth Lafon, 2016

British Library Cataloguing-in-Publication Data
A catalogue record for this book is available from the British Library.
Library of Congress Cataloguing-in-Publication data has been applied for.

ISBN:
HB: 978-1-4088-5556-0
ePub: 978-1-4088-5557-7

2 4 6 8 10 9 7 5 3 1

Designer: Georgia Vaux
Photographer: Jonathan Kennedy
Food stylist: Emily Jonzen
Prop stylist: Cynthia Inions
Illustrator: Babeth Lafon
Indexer: Hilary Bird

Printed and bound in China by RR Donnelley

Bloomsbury Publishing Plc makes every effort to ensure that papers used in the manufacture of our books are natural, recyclable products made from wood grown in well-managed forests. Our manufacturing processes conform to the environmental regulations of the country of origin.

To find out more about our authors and books visit www.bloomsbury.com. Here you will find extracts, author interviews, details of forthcoming events and the option to sign up for our newsletters.

Foggia

Vieste

Adriatic
Sea

Molfetta
Bari

Ostuni

Taranto

Lecce

Puglia

ABRUZZO

MOLISE

CAMPANIA

BASILICATA

(ADRIA...)

Introduction

It was during one of our family's dinnertime gatherings, around a bowl of lentil soup, that my daughter Eleonora looked up to me with a smile and said: 'Thank you, *Mammissima!*' Lentil soup is a simple dish, yet for her it meant the best of home... and with that word, this book began.

I'm a working mum who believes that cooking every day for my family is always worth the effort. This book will show you how fresh, simple food can bring Southern Italian sunshine and flavours to your home, on weekdays as well as at weekends.

I was born in Puglia, the 'heel' of Italy, only a short sail from Greece across the Adriatic Sea. For generations, my family has lived in Molfetta, near Bari, a medieval port and thriving fishing town whose ancient walled *borgo* is itself shaped like a fishbone.

Puglia is a region full of natural beauties and blessed with mild weather throughout the year. Its seas offer an abundance of fish and seafood, and its fertile land produces a wealth of fruit and vegetables such as olives, figs, wheat, almonds and grapes, used to make our celebrated oils, wines, pastas and sweets.

Olive trees in particular mean home to me: every time I am about to land in Bari, their twisted, knotted trunks, their artistically bent, gracious shapes seem to welcome me back. Olive oil runs in the blood of every true-born Puglian and is the cornerstone of our cuisine. Used instead of butter, it gives a delicate taste to our soups, pastas and salads, and is essential in the production of vegetable preserves, from sun-dried tomatoes, artichokes and aubergines to peppers and the formidably spicy *pric o prac* pickle.

As in the rest of Southern Italy, Puglian life centres around the family and its rituals. My childhood recollections are rich with memories of flavours. We'd gather around the table, all of us orbiting the feast – a steaming bowl of orecchiette pasta, a warm, herby focaccia, a glistening pot of octopus stew.

My grandmother used to get us all to help in making passata, the sieved tomato purée that is fundamental to our cuisine. She would buy an industrial quantity of San Marzano plum tomatoes from local farmers, especially if their land was near the coast, as she wanted the tomatoes to have some of the fragrance of the sea. They were washed and boiled, then passed through a sieve grinder. The tomato juice was poured into thoroughly cleaned glass bottles, and sometimes herbs and spices were added. The bottles were hermetically sealed, then wrapped in sheets of newspaper to protect the glass from the heat and placed inside metal drums for boiling. After an hour's cooking, they were taken out and left to cool in large plastic tubs full of water. Then we had homemade sauce that would last throughout the year.

Although I left all that behind when I moved to Britain over fifteen years ago, I was able to recreate part of the food of my homeland with my new family: my husband Alessandro, himself a keen cook, and our children Eleonora and Emiliano, who are now thirteen and ten years old.

Cooking is how you keep traditions alive, and it is a focal point and unifying element of family life. Food instils culture through small, everyday pleasures; it's the smell of supper cooking while the children are doing their homework. When I cook spaghetti with roasted tomatoes or other dishes they love, they race into the kitchen, already knowing what will be on the table. Such scents and flavours become familiar and make us feel that we are at home: 'This is what I recognise – this is what I like.'

And beyond the importance of culture, good food helps your children to grow and develop well. You always want to offer what is best for your children. That is Nature; that is love. The greater the variety of foods that children eat, the better – a varied diet is part of the secret to a healthy life. The challenging thing is to mix something that they don't know or like into something that they do. But, in general, children are curious. So if you present something new in an attractive way, they might give it a go: they might say it's disgusting, but at least you've tried. Or they might say it's fantastic and ask for more. On the whole, freshness and diet are largely a question of habit; once children are used to high-quality food, why would they want something that's less delicious?

To get children to eat well, mammas have to be inventive. It's true that, with all the pressures and commitments of modern living, spending enough time in the kitchen can be a challenge. This book is intended for busy parents like me who have little time on their hands but still want to give their family delicious, healthy food.

Puglian cuisine lends itself perfectly to this, since it's light, warm and nutritious. It is a treasure trove of recipes that children tend to love and which, thanks to their rustic nature, are extremely simple to prepare. From spaghetti with green beans to stuffed peppers and fish soup, these dishes brim with all the natural flavour and wholesome quality of Mediterranean life. They are the authentic meals of the Italian family table – slightly adapted at times so that you can find the ingredients more easily here.

Putting together these recipes has enabled me to rediscover an important part of the cultural heritage of my region. Behind every list of ingredients there is always a rich personal and collective story, because through food we express who we are and where we come from. I hope this book will not only give you some inspiration in the kitchen but also encourage you to reconnect with your own roots and food culture.

Apart from anything else, I want to show that cooking, far from being a chore, can be fun even for a modern parent – especially if you involve the whole family in your culinary mischief.

Note that most of the recipes in this book feed two adults and two children, but they can easily be adapted to feed more people or bigger appetites.

Buon appetito a tutti!

Shopping Guide

Using the right ingredients is essential for the success of your dishes – all the ingredients listed below and throughout the book are widely available.

Olive oil

There are many different kinds of olive oil, so it is important that you know your way around when choosing, and that you use only extra-virgin olive oil, which is produced without any additional chemical treatment and has the best taste. Good-quality, fresh olive oil made from early-harvested olives has a green-yellow colour; it is preferable to buy this in tin cans or dark glass bottles rather than in clear glass or plastic bottles, as olive oil doesn't like light and can oxidise, turning yellow and rancid. One simple rule of thumb is never to go for the cheapest olive oil on the shelves.

Make sure the olive oil you buy comes from Italy (olive oil from Spain and other Mediterranean countries can be of inferior quality due to higher acidity, and differences in climate and production processes). Ideally, the location of the mill and of where the olive oil has been bottled should be the same.

Unlike wine, olive oil does not improve with age, but will retain its flavour and properties for only a limited amount of time. Although it remains edible after the recommended use-by date, olive oil should be consumed within around eighteen months of the date it was produced. So always check the 'date of pressing' – if there is one – on your bottle.

In the old days, olive oil was given to sick children and was regarded as a precious medicine. For that reason, spilling it was considered, as my grandmother used to say, '*una disgrazia*' – many years of guaranteed bad luck.

Pasta

I use both dried and fresh pasta, depending on what I am cooking. As it is quite time-consuming, I tend to make my own fresh pasta at the weekend or on special occasions. For dried pasta, Italian is best. All pasta is relatively inexpensive, and the good brands, whilst costing just a little more, keep their texture better and make a difference. Cheap pasta can be gluey and tasteless.

Unless otherwise stated, the pasta used in the recipes that follow is dried. If you are using shop-bought fresh pasta instead, cut down the cooking time, as instructed on the packet.

As well as familiar shapes such as penne, fusilli and spaghetti, look for small pasta such as stelline, ditalini, chifferi and farfalline, which are perfect for babies and toddlers. I use them in soups or mixed with boiled pulses and peas. As an alternative, you can also break up long pasta such as spaghetti or vermicelli.

It's also worth keeping an eye out for orecchiette, which literally translates as 'little ears' pasta. Frequently used in Puglian dishes, it is becoming widely available in the UK.

Tomatoes

Tomatoes are an essential part of Italian cooking. The recipes in this book make use of cherry tomatoes, the larger 'vine' tomatoes and beef tomatoes. I recommend buying cherry and vine tomatoes loose rather than pre-packed, as they are more tasty and flavourful. If you buy them from a local market, even better. Beef tomatoes must be big, firm and not too ripe. Try to buy them from your local market or a trusted greengrocer's; supermarket beef tomatoes often taste like rainwater.

Passata

I recommend using plain Italian organic passata (sieved, puréed tomatoes) without any added garlic, herbs or other flavourings.

Potatoes

There is a large variety of potatoes to choose from, and some are more appropriate than others for a particular use. On the whole, red-skinned potatoes are good for roasting, soups and mashing. White or more yellow-fleshed potatoes with a firm, waxy or smooth texture (such as Charlotte) are perfect for grilling, boiling and salads. Those with a more floury or fluffy texture (such as King Edward or Maris Piper), sometimes referred to as baking potatoes or all-purpose potatoes, are best for mashing, as well as baking. Sweet potatoes are also great for baking.

Artichokes

The best kind of artichokes to use for the recipes in this book are the small Italian, French or Sardinian ones. They must be as fresh as possible – just look at the leaves, which should be crisp and taut. For directions on how to prepare artichokes, see page 24.

The large 'globe' artichokes you find in supermarkets are not so good for these recipes, as they are too hard, spiky and hairy inside.

Lemons

Where the zest of a lemon is required for a recipe, you should always use unwaxed lemons.

Fish

Before a fish is filleted, have a good long look at it. See if its flesh is firm and elastic. Examine its eyes (which should be bright) and the colour of its gills (which should be red).

If you're buying salmon, try to go for wild or organic salmon rather the standard farmed fish, which can be mass-produced and contain growth hormones and colouring agents.

As my father says, always sniff fish – even through the packaging – as your nose is the best quality controller.

Mince or ground meat

Try to avoid pre-packed mince if you can. It is always preferable to choose a piece of meat from the counter and get a butcher to grind it for you. Choose a leaner cut that is not too fatty: the taste will be fresher and the meat less watery in the pan.

Eggs

The eggs in these recipes are always free-range.

Parmesan

Parmesan cheese is sweet and made of cow's milk, and it can be added to many dishes to give extra flavour. If possible, always buy an authentic Parmigiano Reggiano cheese rather than one of its cheaper imitations, and grate it as needed.

Pecorino Romano

This is a hard, salty cheese made of ewe's milk. It is often used in Puglian cuisine to complement the sweeter taste of Parmesan, or as an addition to dishes with sweet or mild-flavoured ingredients.

Salt

Rock salt and sea salt are tastier than ordinary table salt – the salt used in the recipes is always flaky sea salt, unless otherwise specified. (Note that as a general rule, salt shouldn't be added to dishes for babies and toddlers.)

Rice

I recommend using carnaroli, Arborio or vialone nano rice for all risotto recipes. These short-grain types of rice provide the perfect creamy risotto, whilst keeping their shape and texture.

Lentils

Check the packet for the country of origin and always buy small Italian or French lentils (the smaller the better). Unfortunately you can't find them in every grocery shop or supermarket, so I suggest you stock up at your nearest delicatessen.

Flour

Use Italian '00' white flour to make pizza, egg-free pasta, bread and focaccia, and durum-wheat flour to make egg pasta. Both of these flours are now more widely available in the UK, and can be found in Italian delicatessens and some supermarkets.

Breadcrumbs

Some delicatessens sell real breadcrumbs, not the chemical-tasting type you find in supermarkets. Breadcrumbs are cheap; you can also make them yourself by blitzing stale bread in a blender, preferably from loaves that are a few days old. It's a good idea to freeze some breadcrumbs in sealable bags so that you always have a supply ready to hand. Don't use seasoned breadcrumbs, as the flavour may then interfere with the taste of your dish.

Pasta

$\mathcal{T}wo$ kinds of flour are commonly used in Italy. Whilst the stretchy qualities of finely sieved '00' white flour make it ideal for bread, pizza and focaccia, pasta is made with yellowish durum-wheat flour. Few people make their own pasta these days – every Puglian town has a fresh-pasta shop, so there is no great incentive to learn the technique. I still love making it, though, and so do my children.

There are over 200 dried and fresh pasta shapes. British shops now offer a wide range of them, but I remember when pasta was still quite a rare commodity… When I first came here as a student in the early Eighties, I stayed with a family in Twickenham. They were extremely nice to me and for a whole week the lady of the house cooked spaghetti for me every day. Then I told her that, well, in Italy we don't eat pasta all the time (lie). Without wanting to slight her cooking abilities – though I must admit her spaghetti was overcooked and resembled glue – I was mightily relieved when the following day I found bangers and mash on my plate.

Making fresh pasta is a precious memory from my childhood. My grandmother used to prepare orecchiette ('little ears') each Saturday afternoon: she would dig a well in the flour, add a pinch of salt and pour in water while mixing. Then she would knead the dough for a good ten to fifteen minutes with her strong, skilful hands. My cousin Roberta and I were always happy to help. Nonna taught us the technique of giving the pasta its unique hat shape. Little tubular pieces of dough were dragged (*strascinate* in the Molfettese dialect) across a wooden board with a blunt-edged knife to give them an uneven surface, ideal for capturing the sauce once cooked. Each orecchietta was then reversed over the thumb to create a hump in the middle. It was an intense two-hour job, ending with my cousin and me using the leftover dough to invent new shapes. You can encourage your children to make pasta too, rolling out lasagna sheets and creating their own shapes with the extra dough.

Some pasta basics. Put plenty of water in a tall, deep pan. Bring to the boil, then add 1 tablespoon of rock or sea salt (or ¾ tablespoon of fine salt) per 3 litres of water. Add the pasta, and stir occasionally to stop it sticking. When you think the pasta is nearly ready, lift a piece out (a claw-shaped scoop is useful for this), and bite to test it. Test every 30 seconds, until the pasta is *al dente* – cooked but still firm. Drain the pasta immediately, mix it with your sauce and serve.

Orecchiette pasta with broccoli

Orecchiette con i broccoli

Serves: 4
Prep & cooking:
   25 mins

This is my own version of one of the most famous Puglian recipes, *orecchiette con le cime di rapa* (orecchiette with broccoli rabe). This vegetable is a bit smelly to cook with – but so what? My father once told me that when he did something naughty as a child, his nonna used to squirt broccoli-rabe water on him, saying, 'Blessed be thou, creature of evil!'

Since broccoli rabe is not easy (though by no means impossible) to find here, I have replaced it with Tenderstem broccoli. My fellow Molfettesi would be horrified at this culinary licence, but I can assure you that the result is every bit as good. Orecchiette pasta is a perfect match with vegetables and recently it has become more popular and widely available in this country.

Sea salt
250g Tenderstem
   broccoli
Olive oil
3–4 tbsp breadcrumbs
1 garlic clove, finely
   chopped
A pinch of chilli flakes
   (optional)
400g orecchiette pasta

Bring a tall panful of water to the boil and add salt. Cut off the lower part of the stem from the broccoli and discard the end, if tough. Chop up the rest of the stem. Cook the tips and chopped stem in the pan for about 8 minutes, or until tender.

Meanwhile, heat up 2 tablespoons of olive oil in a frying pan and add the breadcrumbs. Stirring occasionally, cook the breadcrumbs for a few minutes until they turn golden-brown, then set aside.

When the broccoli is nearly ready, heat up 1 tablespoon of olive oil in a large frying pan. Sauté the garlic until it starts to turn brown, stirring occasionally to stop it burning.

Using a skimmer or slotted spoon, transfer the broccoli to the frying pan with the garlic (set the water aside). Mix in the chilli flakes, if using. Cook on a low heat for 5 minutes, stirring occasionally.

Cook the pasta in the broccoli water for 10 minutes, or until *al dente*.

Drain the pasta (reserving a ladleful of cooking water) and mix with the broccoli. Add the breadcrumbs and cook for a couple of minutes more on a low heat, stirring in the reserved pasta water. Serve while still hot, with a dash of olive oil, if you like.

Mamma says

Whenever I am cooking this dish for a group of adults or children who are keen on stronger flavours, I add about 4 fillets of salty-tasting anchovy to the recipe.

If the anchovies are preserved in salt, make sure that they are thoroughly washed and desalted before you use them.

Prepare the recipe in the usual way, following the method opposite.

While the garlic is frying, add the anchovy fillets to the frying pan. Crush the fillets until you get a nice paste, then add the chilli flakes.

Finish the dish as usual, cooking the pasta and mixing it together with the other ingredients.

Spaghetti with roasted tomatoes

Spaghetti con i pomodori al forno

Serves: 4
Prep & cooking:
  15–20 mins

I am particularly fond of this dish, as it was one of my first kitchen experiments. I saw my mamma making it many times when I was a child, especially during the summer holidays when we were all hungry and desperate to eat after coming back from the seaside. Every time I prepare it now, the bright colours of the Puglian beach come to my mind.

Whenever my son Emiliano comes prowling around the kitchen like a little, hungry wolf and asks what we are going to eat, the words '*spaghetti con i pomodori al forno*' never fail to elicit a wide smile. Light and healthy, this dish takes only 15 minutes to prepare.

Olive oil
300g cherry tomatoes, halved
3 sprigs of flat parsley leaves, finely chopped
2 basil leaves, finely chopped
1 garlic clove, finely chopped
70g small pancetta cubes (about 1cm)
2 tsp capers
Sea salt
1 tbsp breadcrumbs
1 tbsp grated Parmesan
250–300g spaghetti

Preheat the oven to 190°C/Gas 5. Spread some olive oil on a ceramic baking dish and lay the tomatoes halves on top, cut-side up. Place all the chopped ingredients in a small bowl and add the pancetta, capers and a pinch of sea salt (not too much, as both capers and pancetta are already quite salty). Stir everything together.

Cover the tomatoes with the mixture and drizzle a little olive oil on top. Sprinkle over the breadcrumbs and Parmesan. Put the dish into the preheated oven and leave for around 12–15 minutes, until the tomatoes soften and are just starting to turn brown.

While the tomatoes are roasting, boil some water for your spaghetti and then add salt. Cook the pasta until *al dente* (about 12 minutes, but check the packet and start testing towards the end of the suggested cooking time). Drain in a colander.

Remove the tomatoes from the oven and toss the pasta into them. Stir briskly for about a minute: your dish will be a steaming-hot masterpiece!

Serve in large shallow bowls; I can assure you your children will forget all about talking – at least for the next 10 minutes or so.

Spaghetti with green beans

Spaghetti con i fagiolini

Serves: 4
Prep & cooking:
 15–20 mins

In Italy, everything can change dramatically if you travel just a few kilometres from your home town. This dish is typical of my area, though there is a similar version in Salento, the southernmost part of Puglia, that uses extra ingredients and follows a different method. In the Salento version, the green beans are cooked in salted water in one pan, while a basic tomato sauce with garlic is prepared in another. The spaghetti is added to the beans to cook at the same time, then both are drained and poured into the pan with the tomato sauce. The dish is served with *cacioricotta*, a cheese produced by local dairies in southern Italy, or *ricotta marzotica*, a Puglian hard ricotta that is usually grated onto pasta.

My *spaghetti con i fagiolini* is a slightly simplified variation, as it doesn't require the preparation of the sauce, and it's always a huge success with the children.

240g green beans,
 trimmed
Fine salt
280g spaghetti
Olive oil
1 garlic clove, finely
 chopped
200g cherry tomatoes,
 halved
A handful of grated
 Parmesan

Tip the green beans into a large pan of boiling salted water and boil for about 4 minutes, or until they are tender but still crisp. Drain well and leave in a bowl.

Bring a deep, tall pan of water to the boil, add salt and cook your spaghetti, stirring occasionally for the first minute or so to prevent sticking. Cook until *al dente* (about 12 minutes, but check the packet and start testing towards the end of the suggested cooking time).

Meanwhile, heat 1 tablespoon of olive oil in a large saucepan and sauté the garlic. Add the cherry tomatoes and a little salt. Cook for a couple of minutes before adding the green beans. Toss everything together with a spoon and dust with the Parmesan.

Once the spaghetti is *al dente*, drain and mix with the green beans and tomatoes. Serve immediately, while still hot.

Mamma says

For younger children, I suggest you break the spaghetti into smaller pieces and purée or chop the green beans.

Pasta salad with raw tomatoes

Pasta alla crudaiola

Serves: 4
Prep & cooking:
  15 mins

I prepare *pasta alla crudaiola* at least once a week at about seven o'clock in the morning, before the children go to school. It's the perfect packed-lunch solution: easy to prepare, fresh, healthy and not too messy.

I am particularly fond of this pasta salad, because it brings out the full flavour of olive oil. For this recipe, most Italians use penne pasta – a versatile pasta that retains all the aroma of the ingredients it's served with, thanks to its shape.

Some of my friends call this dish *pasta bandiera*, as it evokes the colours of the Italian flag. Whatever the name, it's a fantastic Mediterranean recipe, ideal for family meals, parties and picnics.

300g cherry tomatoes, chopped
20g pine kernels
1 garlic clove, finely chopped
6 basil leaves, roughly chopped
Sea salt
300g penne pasta
Olive oil

Place the cherry tomatoes in a bowl. Add the pine kernels, garlic and basil and mix together.

Bring a deep, tall pan of water to the boil, add salt and then the pasta. Cook until *al dente* (about 12 minutes, but check the packet and start testing towards the end of the suggested cooking time).

Drain, then tip into the bowl with the other ingredients. Add about 2 tablespoons of olive oil and mix. Your pasta salad is ready! It can be served at once, or else left to cool for later.

Mamma says

This recipe is extremely simple, but the freshness of the garlic is paramount to its success. There is nothing worse than stale, sprouting or browning garlic for ruining your dish.

Because of possible food allergies, many schools ban nuts; if you are preparing this dish for your children's packed lunch, I suggest replacing the pine kernels with pitted black olives.

Carbonara with artichokes and courgettes

Carbonara di carciofi e zucchine

Serves: 4
Prep & cooking:
  20 mins

My husband sometimes comes home with wonderful Sardinian artichokes, which he buys from a local greengrocer. Although these small artichokes are quite spiky, they are extremely tender on the inside.

This dish is very easy to make and was originally suggested to me by my sister-in-law – another busy, resourceful working mamma – who maintained that it is perfect for children. It didn't take me very long to find out that she was absolutely right. My sister-in-law usually uses spaghetti for this dish, though pappardelle is good too, because the flatter shape works so well with the chunky vegetables.

4 small Italian or
  French artichokes
A little lemon juice or
  white wine vinegar
Olive oil
¼ onion, sliced
50g pancetta cubes
Sea salt
1 courgette, cut into
  2cm dice
250g spaghetti or
  pappardelle
1 egg
A handful of grated
  Pecorino Romano

Cut the stems off the artichokes, then peel off the outer, harder leaves until you get to the tender leaves inside. Be extra careful if they are thorny. Trim off any small leaves from the base and chop off about 4cm from the top of the artichokes – discard the trimmings and all the leaves. Place in a bowl and cover with hot water from the kettle, adding a squeeze of lemon or a dash of vinegar. This will soften the artichokes and take the bitterness away, as well as preventing discolouration. Leave in the bowl for about 3 minutes.

Now drain the artichokes carefully, squeezing out any remaining water. Cut them vertically into slices 1–2cm thick.

Heat 1 tablespoon of olive oil in a frying pan over a medium heat. Add the onion and cook until translucent, stirring occasionally.

Add the pancetta to the onion, along with a pinch of sea salt. Then add the courgette and the artichoke slices. Cover the frying pan with a lid and continue to cook over a medium-low heat for about 15 minutes, stirring now and then.

Meanwhile, cook your pasta. Pour plenty of water into a deep, tall pan and bring to the boil. Add salt. Cook the pasta until *al dente* (about 12 minutes, but check the packet and start testing towards the end of the suggested cooking time).

Continues overleaf

While the pasta is cooking, crack the egg into a bowl and whisk it. Mix in the grated cheese.

Drain the pasta, reserving a ladleful of the hot cooking water (about 150ml).

Mix the pasta with the fried ingredients. Pour the egg mixture in too and stir briskly for about 10 seconds, adding some of the reserved cooking water to loosen the sauce, if needed. Serve the pasta while it's still steaming hot.

Mamma says

If your children are allergic to eggs or you are not comfortable giving them raw eggs, there is an egg-free alternative using ricotta and milk instead.

Prepare the vegetables, pancetta and pasta as normal. Instead of making an egg mixture, tip 100g ricotta into a bowl and mix it with some milk (roughly 50ml) until you get a creamy mixture. Add some grated Pecorino (or Parmesan) and, if you like, season with black pepper. Use this in place of the whisked egg mixture when you finish the dish.

Gnocchi with courgette pesto

Gnocchi con pesto alle zucchine

Serves: 4
Prep & cooking:
　15 mins

Pesto is a staple of Italian cuisine. It's easy to make, healthy and cheap. I always make more than I need, storing some in the fridge or freezer for emergency meals during the week, or for early-morning packed-lunch crises. Our children love pasta with pesto, and prefer this homemade version to the one from supermarkets, which they say is too strong and 'garlicky'.

What makes my Puglian pesto different from the traditional Genoese recipe, apart from avoiding the garlic and using almonds as well as pine kernels, is the use of courgettes. Courgette pesto goes very well with gnocchi – soft durum-wheat pasta dumplings, usually made with potatoes, egg and nutmeg in Puglia – as the two delicate flavours enhance each other beautifully. Because of its subtle, sophisticated taste, this dish is always a great success at dinner parties.

200g courgettes
125ml olive oil, plus
　extra for frying
¼ onion, sliced
Fine salt
10g blanched almonds
10g (a small bunch)
　basil leaves
30g pine kernels
50g Pecorino Romano
500g gnocchi

Slice the courgettes into rounds 3–4mm thick, removing the ends.

Heat some olive oil in a frying pan over a medium heat and add the onion, courgettes and a pinch of fine salt. Cook, stirring occasionally, for 5 minutes.

Place the almonds, basil, pine kernels, Pecorino, 125ml olive oil and ½ teaspoon of fine salt in a blender, then add the courgettes and onion, and whizz until you get a smooth pesto sauce.

Bring a deep, tall pan of water to the boil, add salt, and cook the gnocchi for 3 minutes or so, until they start rising to the surface. Drain in a colander and mix with the courgette pesto before serving.

Mamma says

This recipe works just as well with other kinds of pasta, such as fusilli and penne. I recommend trying baby courgettes for the pesto sauce, as they have an even milder flavour.

Pasta with chickpeas

Pasta e ceci

Serves: 4
Prep: 15 mins
Cooking: 1 hour

This dish, one of the simplest and most delicious dishes in Puglian cuisine, is perhaps a legacy from the time when the Arabs dominated our region back in the ninth century. As testified by the popularity of hummus throughout the Middle East and North Africa, Arabs still love chickpeas – and so do the people of Puglia.

200g dried chickpeas
Sea salt
3 sprigs of rosemary
1 carrot, peeled and cut into large chunks
1 celery stalk, cut into large chunks
2 garlic cloves, peeled
12 cherry tomatoes, halved
Olive oil
250g small pasta (such as chifferi, broken spaghetti, ditalini or conchiglie)
Black pepper (optional)

Soak the chickpeas in slightly salted water overnight.

Drain, rinse and tip into a saucepan of fresh cold water. Bring to the boil, so that a white foam rises. Drain and rinse the chickpeas.

Boil some water in the kettle, then pour into the pan. Bring the water back to the boil, then tip in the chickpeas and cook for 15 minutes, covering partially with a lid.

Add the rosemary, carrot, celery, garlic, tomatoes, a large pinch of salt and 1 tablespoon of olive oil. Leave to cook for another 45 minutes, or until the chickpeas become soft.

Meanwhile, bring a deep, tall pan of well-salted water to the boil and cook the pasta until *al dente* (check the packet and start testing towards the end of the cooking time), stirring now and then.

Drain the pasta (reserving the cooking water) and place it in shallow bowls. Drain the chickpeas, discarding the vegetables. Add the chickpeas to the pasta with enough reserved pasta water to make a sauce. Season with a little black pepper, if you like, and serve.

Mamma says

If you're in a rush, just use tinned chickpeas. Drain and rinse the chickpeas. As above, tip into a saucepan with the other ingredients (for extra flavour, add half a vegetable stock cube). Cook for around 30 minutes, until the chickpeas soften, and serve with the pasta.

Any leftover chickpeas will keep for two days in the fridge: for a quick lunch, take them out and cook extra pasta as needed.

Spaghetti with breadcrumbs

Spaghetti con pangrattato

Serves: 4
Prep & cooking:
  15 mins

One summer holiday, I was at the beach with friends, having one of our usual conversations about husbands. One friend said: 'So I left him on his own for a whole week, and the only thing he could cook was spaghetti with breadcrumbs.' Well, I was intrigued by this confession; I knew that her husband would find boiling an egg a challenge and always paid a little visit to his mamma's house at lunchtime when he was alone. So just how easy could this recipe be if one of the most slothful men in town wasn't daunted by it? I moved the conversation on to the cooking instructions.

Since then, *spaghetti con pangrattato* has become one of the most popular recipes in our household. I cook it when the fridge is empty and our children start hovering around me asking for food. As my friend said, 'If my husband can do it, everyone can do it!'

Sea salt
350g spaghetti
Olive oil
A pinch of chilli flakes
2 garlic cloves, finely
  chopped
160g breadcrumbs

Bring plenty of water to the boil in a deep, tall pan, then add salt. Add the spaghetti, stirring to prevent sticking. Cook until *al dente* (about 12 minutes, but check the packet and start testing towards the end of the suggested cooking time).

Meanwhile, heat 1 tablespoon of olive oil in a frying pan. Add the chilli flakes and half of the garlic, then sauté for about a minute.

In a separate frying pan, heat 2 tablespoons of olive oil on a medium heat, then add the remaining garlic and the breadcrumbs. Stir until the breadcrumbs are brown and crunchy.

Drain the cooked spaghetti and add to the breadcrumbs. Mix in the sautéed garlic and serve while still hot.

Mamma says

If your children like anchovies, you can add them to the garlic and chilli flakes, giving a bit of extra flavour to the dish.

Chilli flakes can be replaced by pepper, which can be ground over before serving. If your children don't like spicy flavours at all, just garnish the spaghetti with finely chopped basil instead.

Stuffed pasta shells

Conchiglioni ripieni

Serves: 4
Prep & cooking:
45 mins

Isabella, my sister-in-law, recommended this recipe for stuffing conchiglioni, or large pasta shells. It's a real hit with her son, who will always ask for more when still chomping away at the first round.

The dish requires a simple tomato sauce based on passata, the sieved tomato purée that is part of many Puglian recipes. In the late summer, my grandmother used to commandeer the entire house and family and embark on one of her carefully regimented passata-making campaigns. Afterwards, every room was so full of bottles of passata that it was impossible for us children to play inside the house. Although hard work, these sauce-making sessions were great fun, and besides being wonderful family occasions, they guaranteed a supply of delicious passata for the whole year ahead.

Sea salt
250g conchiglioni pasta
200g lean beef mince
1 egg
1 x mozzarella (125g), diced
3–4 tbsp grated Parmesan

For the tomato sauce
Olive oil
½ onion, finely sliced
250ml passata
250g tinned plum tomatoes
1 celery stalk, finely chopped
1 small carrot, finely chopped
4 basil leaves, torn
Sea salt

To prepare the tomato sauce, heat up 1 tablespoon of olive oil in a saucepan over a medium heat. Add the onion and leave it to sizzle until it becomes translucent, then pour in the passata and tinned tomatoes. Add the celery, carrot and basil. Season with a little salt. Pour in 150ml water, cover, bring to the boil and then turn down the heat. Partially cover with a lid and simmer for 20 minutes. Taste and add more salt if necessary.

Meanwhile, bring a deep, tall pan of water to the boil, then add salt. Cook the pasta for about 3 minutes (or about half the cooking time recommended on the packet). Drain and put to one side.

Preheat the oven to 190°C/Gas 5. In a bowl, mix the mince, egg, mozzarella and a little salt. Then fill each pasta shell with the mixture – about 1 teaspoon in each shell.

Cover the bottom of a baking dish with a layer of tomato sauce. Lay the stuffed shells in the dish in a single layer and cover with more tomato sauce and some grated Parmesan. Put in the oven for about 20–25 minutes, until the cheese is patched with brown. Serve warm.

Spaghetti with fresh clams

Spaghetti alle vongole veraci

Serves: 4
Prep & cooking:
  15–20 mins

In my experience, children like clams more than mussels, and the combination with spaghetti is just perfect. This recipe is one of the centrepieces of Puglian cuisine, and my family's favourite version is made by the Adriatico, a waterfront seafood restaurant in my hometown of Molfetta. The tables are arranged on a platform that looks out directly over the sea, and if you go in the evening you can see the glimmering lights coming from the fishermen's boats in the distance; the fish are attracted by the light, which they mistake for sunlight, making them easier to catch.

My husband Alessandro is a real maestro of this recipe. As a publisher, he has a long track record of bribing authors into signing book contracts after a generous portion of *spaghetti alle vongole veraci* and an excellent bottle of white wine. Perhaps it is no coincidence that we also enjoyed a memorable *spaghettata* – as we call a spaghetti meal – on the day he asked me to marry him.

500g clams
Olive oil
2 garlic cloves, finely chopped
½ shallot, chopped
15 cherry tomatoes, chopped
Chilli flakes (optional)
2 tbsp white wine or ½ tbsp white wine vinegar
A handful of flat parsley leaves, roughly chopped
Sea salt
300g spaghetti

First of all, wash the clams carefully and repeatedly under fresh water to flush away the grit. Discard any that are cracked or are open and don't close when tapped.

Cover the bottom of a deep pan or wok with a generous quantity of olive oil (about 5 tablespoons). Place the clams inside and add the garlic. Add the shallot, tomatoes and some chilli flakes (if using). Sprinkle with the white wine or white wine vinegar, then add the parsley and season with sea salt.

Mix together the contents of your pan or wok, cover with a lid and cook on a medium heat for about 10 minutes, until your clams are all opened and well cooked, stirring once or twice during cooking. Discard any clams that remain closed.

Meanwhile, cook the spaghetti. Bring to the boil plenty of water in a deep, tall pan. Add salt, then the pasta, and cook until *al dente* (about 12 minutes, but check the packet and start testing towards the end of the suggested cooking time), stirring occasionally to prevent sticking.

Drain the pasta in a colander set over the sink. Toss the pasta into the clams and keep stirring for another minute or so on a low heat. The key to the success of this recipe is timing, so don't leave it too long, and serve the dish steaming hot.

Mamma says

I would always recommend buying the freshest clams that you can lay your hands on. Ask your local fishmonger when they have their clams delivered and make sure to buy them on that day.

   Alternatively, you can order online for a direct delivery from the coast. It's a bit more expensive, but a guarantee of quality and freshness.

Penne pasta with salmon

Penne al salmone

Serves: 4
Prep & cooking:
 20 mins

This is a quick recipe I turn to when I am totally zonked out and I don't feel like spending too much time in the kitchen. My husband and our children love it, so I know I mustn't feel too guilty about it, especially as salmon is a very healthy ingredient, one I have heard described as a 'nutritional marvel'.

Since I moved to Britain, salmon has become one of my favourite foods, both fresh and smoked. I have seen several versions of this dish – some with brandy and cherry tomatoes – but I prefer this simple one with white wine and parsley, as it is both easy to make and full of flavour.

Olive oil
1 shallot, finely sliced
120g smoked salmon, shredded
A splash of white wine
200ml crème fraîche
3 sprigs of flat parsley leaves, finely chopped
Sea salt
300g penne pasta

Pour plenty of water into a deep pan and bring it to the boil.

Meanwhile, heat about 1 tablespoon of olive oil in a frying pan over a medium heat and sauté the shallot until it is translucent. Add the smoked salmon and sprinkle in the white wine. Stir with a wooden spoon for a few minutes, until the salmon turns light pink. Add the crème fraîche and the chopped parsley. Cook for another 5 minutes, always stirring, then take off the heat and set aside.

Once the water has reached the boil, add salt and the pasta. Leave to cook until *al dente* (about 12 minutes, but check the packet and start testing towards the end of the suggested cooking time).

Drain the pasta, reserving a couple of ladlefuls of cooking water. Return the pasta to the pan and mix in the salmon and the other ingredients, adding some of the reserved water to moisten if needed. Serve while steaming hot, as the salmon sauce does have a tendency to dry up quickly.

Mamma says

Farfalle pasta works equally well for this recipe. For the salmon, I'd advise using a mild-smoked variety, as children tend to prefer more delicate flavours.

Oven-baked pasta

Pasta al forno

Serves: 6
Prep: 30 mins
Cooking: 25–30 mins

For this dish – known in our Molfettese dialect as *méccarauene o furne* – maccheroni pasta (or its variant tortiglioni) is most commonly used, but I prefer to use penne instead.

Pasta al forno often appears on our table at Sunday lunches when we are on holiday in Molfetta, and its smell wafts through the moment I open the door after a late-morning aperitivo. After *pasta al forno* followed by fruit and dessert, everyone is ready to lie down for at least three hours. Between two and five in the afternoon, even on weekdays, everything seems to be asleep in Molfetta. Now you may guess the reason.

Fine salt
500g penne pasta
150g grated Parmesan
1 x mozzarella (125g),
  drained and diced
1 slice of mortadella
  (25g), shredded

For the meatballs
500g lean beef mince
Olive oil
1 garlic clove, chopped
1 small onion, sliced

For the tomato sauce
500ml passata
1 x 400g tin plum
  tomatoes
1 celery stalk,
  finely chopped
1 carrot, finely chopped
3 sprigs of flat
  parsley leaves,
  roughly chopped
Sea salt

First prepare the meatballs. Roll the mince into little balls about the size of a walnut in its shell. Heat up 1 tablespoon of olive oil in a large saucepan or sauté pan on a medium heat. Add the garlic and onion and cook for a minute or so, stirring occasionally, until the onion becomes translucent. Put the meatballs in the saucepan and cook until browned all over.

Next, make the tomato sauce. Pour the passata and the tinned tomatoes into the pan, then add the celery, carrot and parsley. Pour in 150ml water, cover with a lid until it boils, and then simmer, half-covered, for about 20 minutes. Season with salt.

Meanwhile, cook the pasta. Bring a deep, tall pan of water to the boil and add salt. Cook your penne for about 12 minutes, or until *al dente*, then drain.

Preheat the oven to 200°C/Gas 6. Cover the bottom of a ceramic baking dish (about 30 x 20cm if rectangular, or 27cm wide if round) with a third of the tomato sauce (leave the meatballs in the pan). Tip in half of the cooked pasta and mix well with the sauce.

Scatter on half of the Parmesan, all the mozzarella and all the mortadella. Crumble some or all of the meatballs (keep some back if your family aren't big meat-eaters) and spread them on top. Layer on half the remaining tomato sauce and the rest of the pasta.

Cover with the rest of the tomato sauce and scatter over the remaining Parmesan. Sprinkle over a little salt and bake for 25 minutes, or until the top has browned.

Serve the oven-baked pasta while still hot.

Mamma says

Our children also love the meatballs on their own in a bit of extra tomato sauce and they always ask for these after a portion of *pasta al forno*, so I tend to set some aside expressly.

If you want to go easy on your family's digestive systems, try to use 'light' mozzarella, as well as lean mince (10% fat or less).

Traditional lasagna

Lasagna tradizionale

Serves: 5–6
Prep & cooking:
about 1 hour 15 mins

In Southern Italy, the most common type of lasagna is the béchamel-free version described below.

My husband Alessandro is an expert lasagna maker, and whenever I feel a bit lazy – which is not as infrequently as you might think – I let him take control of the cooking. One evening, when we had made lasagna for some Puglian friends, everyone was full of compliments – and later my friend Claudia asked jokingly if I could lend her Alessandro from time to time. I glanced at Mauro, her husband, who shrugged and said with a smile: 'Italians are a people of food swingers.'

250g lean beef mince
Olive oil
½ onion, sliced
1 tsp white wine
  vinegar
1 litre passata
Sea salt
16 lasagna sheets,
  fresh or dried
50g grated Parmesan
  (or 100g if you don't
  have Pecorino
  Romano)
50g grated Pecorino
  Romano (or 100g
  if you don't have
  Parmesan)
2 x mozzarelle (250g),
  diced

Preheat the oven to 180°C/Gas 4. Roll the mince into little balls (about the size of a walnut in its shell).

Heat up 1 tablespoon of olive oil in a large saucepan over a medium heat and sauté the sliced onion until translucent. Next, place the meatballs in the pan and cook until brown, turning over carefully with a wooden spoon. Sprinkle with the vinegar. Leave to cook for 2–3 minutes, then add the passata and 700ml water, and season with salt. Simmer for 20–25 minutes, stirring now and then.

Remove 3 of the meatballs to a plate and leave the rest in the sauce.

Next, bring a deep, tall pan of water to the boil, add salt, then dip a quarter of the lasagna sheets in the boiling water, 2–3 sheets at a time. Remove after 1 minute for fresh lasagne, 2 for dry. Lay on a clean, dry tea towel to cool for at least 30 seconds.

Spread the base of a ceramic baking dish (about 30 x 20cm) evenly with a layer of meatball sauce, then cover with a layer of the cooked lasagne sheets – don't worry if they overlap.

Using some of the remaining meatball sauce, cover the sheets with a new layer of sauce.

Scatter on a quarter of the grated Parmesan and Pecorino, and a quarter of the diced mozzarella.

Meanwhile, dip another quarter of the lasagna sheets in the boiling water. Use them to form a new layer.

Again, cover the lasagna sheets with sauce, then scatter on a quarter more Parmesan, Pecorino and mozzarella.

Repeat the above instructions for two more layers, until you have formed four layers in total; crumble the 3 reserved whole meatballs under the final layer of cheese.

Place the dish in the oven and bake for 35–40 minutes, or until the pasta is cooked and the top of the lasagna is brown.

Mamma says

The leftover meatball sauce can be used the following day to make a quick pasta meal, so don't throw anything away. Since this recipe requires quite a bit of work, I suggest you keep it for the weekend, especially if you're planning to make your own pasta sheets.

For a special school lunch, during the run-up to Christmas for example, I prepare lasagna in the evening and cook it first thing the following morning. It's a spectacle to see Emiliano's face when he wakes up to the smell of lasagna: there's nothing more delicious you can put in your children's packed lunch.

Homemade pasta

Pasta fatta in casa

Makes: 600g pasta
Prep: 15 mins, plus
  rolling time
Resting: 30 mins

My grandmother was a real expert in this field. In her kitchen, there were a dozen rolling pins of varying length and thickness. She knew exactly which one to use when – I think she was born with a rolling pin in her hand. Once I saw her using five different ones while she was rolling out the pasta. I asked her why she kept changing them, and her answer was, 'Because this is how you do it.' Although it's not something that keeps me awake at night, I still regard this as one of the greatest mysteries surrounding pasta.

Pasta-making is a fun activity to do with children. There are two main types to choose from: with or without egg. Egg pasta is richer, and I usually make it on Sundays and special occasions – it also cooks slightly more quickly.

For egg pasta
400g durum-wheat
  flour, plus extra for
  dusting
2 teaspoons fine salt
4 eggs

For egg-free pasta
400g '00' white flour,
  plus extra for dusting
2 teaspoons fine salt
1 tablespoon olive oil
  (optional)

Pile the flour on a clean work surface. Create a large well in the centre and add the salt. If you are making egg pasta, crack the eggs into the well and beat them gently with a fork, starting to mix them with the flour as you do so. For egg-free pasta, use the same method but pour 170ml warm water into the well instead of the eggs. You can also add 1 tablespoon of olive oil together with the water to help make this egg-free dough more pliable and easier to roll.

Once the liquid is roughly mixed with the flour near the centre of the well, use your hands to pile the rest of the flour into the centre and gradually incorporate until well combined.

Knead the dough by pushing it away from you with the base of your palm, folding it back, pushing it away, then folding it back again. Turn the dough 90 degrees and repeat the same movement until, after about 10 minutes, you get a smooth ball of dough. Wrap the dough in cling film and refrigerate for 30 minutes before using.

You can also use a mixer to make the dough, but you will still have to knead it with your hands for a few minutes to develop the gluten (the substance which gives it an elastic texture), so that the pasta won't come out flabby and it will cook *al dente*.

Continues overleaf

To achieve the perfect thickness, I use a pasta machine. Secure your pasta machine to the work surface and remove the dough from the fridge. Dust your work surface with flour. Take a lump of dough the size of an apple (set the rest of the dough aside, wrapped in cling film) and press it out flat, then roll it to about 2mm thick with a rolling pin. Use a pizza cutter or knife to cut your dough sheet into rectangles narrow enough to go through the machine.

Feed the rectangles through the machine, at the right setting to get a medium thickness. You may have to fold the pasta in two and feed it through again a couple of times to get a smooth and even sheet. Each pasta machine has different settings, so I suggest you start with the medium setting and then work your way down the notches until you are happy with the thickness of the pasta coming out. The final thickness you should be aiming at depends on the kind of pasta: if it's tagliatelle, 1.5mm is about right, whereas stuffed pasta such as tortellini or ravioli need to be 1mm thick; lasagne sheets should be 0.5mm – or as thin as possible without tearing. You may have to repeat the folding and feeding operations a few times at each stage. If you are making egg-free pasta, I suggest you dust your dough regularly with a little bit of flour as you roll, in order to prevent it from sticking.

Cut the dough into rectangles, if using for lasagna. If you are making long pasta, such as tagliatelle, fit the relevant accessory onto your machine and roll the sheet through the machine again, this time cutting it into long strands.

Dust flour on both sides of your fresh pasta and leave it to dry on clean tea towels for 25–30 minutes before using. Repeat the entire rolling, cutting and drying process with the rest of the dough.

Mamma says

You can make the pasta dough in advance: refrigerate it overnight, wrapped in cling film. You can also freeze the dough, wrapped in cling film and foil. Defrost and then roll out the pasta as usual.

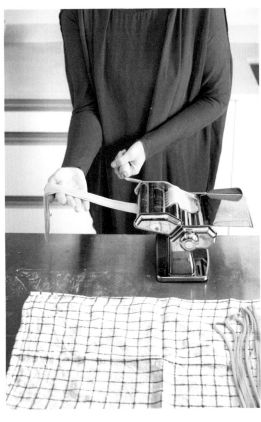

Risotto and Soup

Rice has been combined with the most diverse ingredients in Puglian food over the course of a long culinary history. In this chapter, I've included a variety of risottos, as they are a favourite with children everywhere.

Rice is trickier to cook than it seems. When using it to make risotto, it's important that you keep stirring all the time if you don't want it to stick to the bottom of the saucepan and get burned. Stirring also helps to distribute the starch and makes the dish creamy. It is true that risotto requires a bit of patience – but it's well worth the trouble. For risottos, I recommend using carnaroli, Arborio or vialone nano rice. These short-grain types of rice absorb the liquid well and create the characteristic texture and appearance of the dish.

A number of Puglian soups are based on pulses. Such legumes are an extremely important component in a child's diet because of their nutritional value. Simple and cheap, for centuries they were the main fare of many families in rural areas of our region. In particular, *fave* (broad beans), were seen as the 'meat of the poor' – and they accompany many traditional Puglian recipes. 'The broad bean is the queen of all legumes,' as an old saying goes.

Soup is a very versatile dish and the classic Italian vegetable soup, *minestrone*, proves this point. Living in London, I happen to meet people who come from many different parts of Italy, and I know that our friends from Milan will add meat or pancetta to their version of the soup, while our Neapolitan friends are likely to use peppers and aubergines. In Puglia, depending on the season, we add traditional vegetables and legumes from our land, such as *fave*, *cime di rapa* (broccoli rabe) and *bietole* (chard). Such flexibility allows you to adapt soups to suit your family's tastes too.

Soup is often a favourite with toddlers and children, who can be introduced to many kinds of vegetables through it; soup is also the perfect comfort food during autumn and winter.

Prawn and lemon risotto

Risotto di gamberi al limone

Serves: 4
Prep & cooking:
40 mins

Our daughter Eleonora was only two years old when she ate this dish for the first time in a restaurant in Molfetta, and I was quite surprised to see how much she enjoyed it. It's an easy recipe, and the delicate flavours make it a guaranteed success with children of all ages. Don't worry about using wine for a dish that is to be served to children, since the alcohol boils away during cooking.

Olive oil
20g unsalted butter
1 small onion, finely
  chopped
300g carnaroli or other
  risotto rice
Finely grated zest
  of 1 lemon
A good splash of white
  wine or ½ tbsp white
  wine vinegar
3 sprigs of flat parsley
  leaves, finely chopped

For the prawns
Olive oil
¼ onion, finely sliced
1 celery stalk, chopped
  into slices up to 5mm
  thick
1 carrot, peeled and
  chopped into slices
  up to 3mm thick
5 cherry tomatoes,
  halved
Sea salt
20 raw shell-on tiger
  prawns

First prepare the prawns. Pour 1 tablespoon of olive oil into a saucepan and add the onion, celery, carrot and cherry tomatoes. Cook over a medium-low heat for 5 minutes.

Now pour 1.4 litres of water into the pan. Bring to the boil, season with about ½ teaspoon of salt and then add the prawns. Turn down the heat and simmer for around 10 minutes.

Transfer the prawns to a plate to cool, then remove the shells – but leave 4 prawns unshelled for garnishing with later. Keep the prawn stock simmering on a low heat. If you like, you can strain off the vegetables to make the stock easier to ladle into the rice, but this is not essential. You should have around 1.2 litres of stock.

In a separate saucepan, heat up another 1 tablespoon of olive oil over a medium-low heat. Add the butter and sauté the finely chopped onion until it becomes translucent.

Add the rice to the sautéed onion and pour over a ladleful of hot prawn stock. Stir until the rice absorbs the liquid, then add the lemon zest and the white wine or white wine vinegar. Pour in another ladleful of stock to cover the rice and keep stirring. Repeat this process, adding the prawns to your risotto after about 10 minutes. Keep stirring for another 7–8 minutes or more, until the rice has absorbed all or most of the stock and becomes creamy but is still firm.

Finish with the chopped parsley and garnish with the 4 unshelled prawns, for a sense of occasion. Serve with bread, if you like.

Mamma says

For a quicker version of the risotto, use cooked, peeled prawns
and vegetable stock. Pour 1 tablespoon of olive oil into a frying pan
then add 1 finely chopped garlic clove and the chopped leaves from
3 parsley sprigs. Sauté for 1 minute over a medium-low heat, then
add 250g cooked, peeled tiger prawns and stir for 3 minutes.

In a saucepan, melt 20g unsalted butter with another 1 tablespoon
of olive oil over a medium-low heat. Sauté ¼ of an onion, finely
chopped, until it is translucent.

Meanwhile, fill another saucepan with 1.2 litres of water and
bring it up to a simmer, adding a vegetable stock cube and stirring to
dissolve it. Now add the risotto rice to the onion and continue as
opposite, using the vegetable stock in place of prawn stock.

Asparagus and carrot risotto

Risotto con carote e asparagi

Serves: 4
Prep & cooking:
  25 mins

Once I saw my friend Lina 'toast' risotto rice by stir-frying it in olive oil and butter with onion and white wine, while adding small amounts of hot vegetable stock. If you listen to purists, this procedure, called *tostatura*, is essential to preserve the rice's texture and firmness, but I favour a quicker and lighter way of cooking risotto – just like my mamma does – which doesn't involve stir-frying the rice. I prefer to use fine asparagus in this recipe, but you can also use the standard size.

200g fine asparagus
½ vegetable stock cube
A knob of unsalted
  butter
½ onion, finely sliced
1 carrot, peeled and
  chopped into slices
  up to 3mm thick
Sea salt
500g carnaroli or other
  risotto rice
1 tbsp grated Parmesan

Cut the woody end off each asparagus stalk and discard. Cut off the tips and roughly chop the rest of the stalks.

Pour 1 litre of water into a pan, then add the stock cube and bring to the boil, stirring to dissolve the stock cube.

Meanwhile, melt the butter in a separate saucepan and cook the onion over a medium-low heat until it becomes translucent and glossy. Add the chopped asparagus and tips, and the carrot. Pour in enough of the stock to cover the vegetables and bring to the boil. Season with sea salt, turn down the heat and simmer for about 5 minutes.

Add the rice to the vegetables in the pan, then pour in a ladleful of stock. Stir slowly and keep adding stock when the rice has absorbed most of the liquid (you might not need all of the stock). After about 18 minutes, or when the rice is *al dente*, add the Parmesan and stir. Serve while the risotto is still steaming-hot.

Rice salad

Insalata di riso

Serves: 4
Prep & cooking:
25 mins

Rice salad is a simple recipe that can be enjoyed hours after it's been cooked without losing any of its flavour. If you're standing on a beach in Puglia during the summer, you will see just how many mammas and nonnas are busy dishing out portions of it to their nearest and dearest under their shady *ombrelloni* at lunchtime.

Ideal for family picnics, rice salad can also be served at parties as an alternative to the more predictable bowl of pasta salad. Children of all ages love it, as do adults, so with one dish you can keep everyone happy.

Because cooked rice can cause food poisoning if left for a long time at room temperature, it is essential that you put the rice salad in the fridge soon after it's cooked if you're not eating it straight away. Make sure you eat the rice salad within 24 hours of cooking.

Sea salt
400g Arborio or other
  risotto rice
4 small frankfurters,
  chopped into 2cm
  pieces
50g sliced Italian
  cooked ham,
  roughly chopped
½ cucumber, sliced
4 vine tomatoes, sliced
1 x mozzarella (125g)
  or smoked scamorza
A knob of butter
80ml olive oil
Juice of ½ lemon

Bring a deep, tall pan of water to the boil, add salt and cook your rice for approximately 15–18 minutes, until it's *al dente*.

Meanwhile, place the chopped meat and vegetables in a bowl. Dice the mozzarella (or scamorza) and mix with the other ingredients in the bowl.

When the rice is ready, drain and tip into the bowl. Add the butter and stir carefully until all the ingredients are well mixed together.

Pour the olive oil into a cup and add the lemon juice. Whisk with a fork and pour it onto the rice salad. Mix gently but well. Let the dish rest for a few minutes before serving.

Mamma says

For a meat-free *insalata di riso*, replace the frankfurters with 2 halved boiled eggs, and the Italian ham with a tin of tuna. For this version, I don't add lemon juice to the rice, as it clashes with the other flavours.

Vegetable soup

Minestrone

Serves: 4
Prep & cooking:
   40–45 mins

Minestrone is an inexpensive soup, usually made from any spare seasonal vegetables – its ingredients, seasoning and consistency vary widely across the twenty Italian regions. My husband, who hails from Genzano, near Rome, likes his *minestrone* with more broth, while my mamma's vegetable soup is thicker and denser in texture. My own version is somewhere in the middle.

Olive oil
¼ onion, finely sliced
350g firm-textured
   potatoes (such as
   Charlotte), cut into
   4cm dice
3 chestnut mushrooms,
   roughly chopped
5 baby courgettes
   (or 1 standard one),
   trimmed and roughly
   chopped
100g fine green beans,
   trimmed and roughly
   chopped
100g peas, ideally
   shelled fresh ones
10 cherry tomatoes,
   halved
2 small cauliflowers,
   roughly chopped
1 celery stalk, roughly
   chopped
1 carrot, roughly chopped
3 sprigs of flat parsley
   leaves, roughly
   chopped
Sea salt
Parmesan (optional)

Heat 1 tablespoon of olive oil in a deep pan over a medium heat and sauté the onion until it becomes translucent.

Add all the vegetables and parsley, pour in 2 litres of cold water, cover with a lid and bring to the boil. Once the water has reached the boil, take the lid off and season with sea salt. Reduce the heat and simmer, with the lid only partially on, for about 30–35 minutes.

If you like, add a generous tablespoon of freshly grated Parmesan 5 minutes before the end of the cooking process. Serve hot.

Mamma says

You can blend the boiled vegetables into a soup to be served with croutons and an abundant sprinkling of Parmesan, thus creating a spin-off dish that is ideal for toddlers and loved by children of all ages.

You can also pour some of the liquid from the soup into ice trays and put these in the freezer. The resulting cubes can be used at a later date as vegetable stock for other recipes such as chicken soup or potato soup.

Lentil soup

Minestra di lenticchie

Serves: 4–6
Prep & cooking:
   40 mins

Lentils can be found in many Mediterranean recipes. A Jordanian friend, who was on his second helping of this soup, once mentioned a similar Palestinian dish called *m'jaddara*. The Arab influence may explain why some of our Puglian *minestre* are thick, whereas elsewhere they are more liquid; children seem to prefer the drier version, and I sometimes drain off the liquid from one portion to make a lentil salad for packed lunch the next day.

Lentils also crop up on every Italian's plate at midnight on New Year's Eve, when *cotechino e lenticchie* (fresh pork sausage with lentils) is served. It is believed that the more lentils you eat, the more money you will make in the new year. If that was true, we'd all be millionaires in our family by now.

Olive oil
½ onion, finely sliced
1 garlic clove, finely
   chopped
1 carrot, finely chopped
1 celery stalk, finely
   chopped
4 cherry tomatoes,
   halved
500g Italian or French
   small green lentils
3 sprigs of flat parsley
   leaves, roughly
   chopped
2 bay leaves
½ vegetable stock cube
Sea salt
1 tbsp grated Parmesan
300g Arborio or other
   risotto rice

In a saucepan, heat up 1 tablespoon of olive oil over a medium heat and sauté the onion and the garlic for a few minutes, then add the carrot, celery, tomatoes and lentils.

Add 2 litres of cold water, cover with a lid and bring to the boil, then take the lid off and add the parsley, bay leaves and stock cube. Season with sea salt. At this point reduce the heat and simmer for about 25–30 minutes, until the lentils are tender and some of the liquid has evaporated. Stir the lentils from time to time and add the Parmesan when they are half-cooked, to give extra flavour.

Meanwhile, bring a deep, tall pan of salted water to the boil and cook the rice until it is *al dente*, then drain it.

Separate the lentils from the rest of the vegetables and add to the rice with some of the broth in which they were boiled. Serve hot.

Mamma says

When puréed, this dish is ideal for babies.

As an alternative to lentils you can try borlotti beans. Remember to soak them in water overnight if you're using dried beans, and replace the bay leaves with one or two small peeled potatoes.

Potato soup

Minestra di patate

Serves: 4
Prep: 10 mins
Cooking: 45 mins

Potato soup is the perfect busy mum's dish: prepared in a large quantity, it can be stored and used more than once. Sometimes – well, often – when I return late from work, I don't feel like cooking, so I just take the pan of soup out of the fridge and heat it up for dinner. All I need to do is boil some pasta or rice to mix in.

You only need 10 minutes' active preparation time, but it takes a while for the potatoes and the other vegetables to give the soup its tasty flavour. Since there's always plenty to do in the house, I use that time to tidy everything up in preparation for the evening meal.

Children love potatoes cooked every which way, so you are guaranteed success with this simple recipe, which is also ideal for babies and toddlers.

Olive oil
½ onion, sliced
2 carrots, peeled
2 celery stalks, finely chopped
500g potatoes (any type), peeled and cut into medium wedges
5–6 tbsp passata
½ vegetable stock cube
Sea salt
150g rice or small pasta (such as stelline, farfalline or broken spaghetti)
Parmesan, to serve

Pour 1 tablespoon of olive oil into a deep, tall pan, and add the onion, carrots, celery, potato and passata. Add 2 litres of cold water, cover with a lid and bring to the boil, then take the lid off, add the stock cube and season with sea salt, to taste. Reduce the heat and simmer for about 45 minutes, stirring now and then.

Meanwhile, bring a saucepan of salted water to the boil and cook the rice or pasta until *al dente* (check the packet and start testing towards the end of the suggested cooking time), then drain. Serve the rice or pasta in shallow bowls and pour the hot soup over it. Sprinkle a little freshly grated Parmesan on top.

Mamma says

If you want to make the soup creamier, use a skimmer to remove the cooked potatoes from the pan, then mash and stir them back into the soup.

If you like, add a piece of Parmesan rind about 10 minutes before the end of the cooking time. This will add extra flavour to your soup. But don't do that if you've invited my husband for dinner: Parmesan is anathema to him, especially with potato soup.

Chicken broth

Brodo di pollo

Serves: 4
Prep: 5 mins
Cooking: 50 mins

Olive oil
½ onion, finely
   chopped
2 carrots, chopped into
   thick slices
1 celery stalk
4–5 tbsp passata
4–6 free-range chicken
   drumsticks or 2 free-
   range chicken legs
½ vegetable stock
   cube
Sea salt
150g taglierini pasta
   (or small pasta such
   as stelline, farfalline,
   tortellini)
1 tbsp grated Parmesan,
   to serve

There's a reason my grandmother used to call chicken soup *u bròete pu mélatiedde*, 'the sick child's soup'. Because of its protein content and easy digestibility, *brodo di pollo* is considered a great remedy for colds, so whenever our children return from school with a sore throat or a blocked nose, I give them a bowl of hot chicken broth. By morning, they are usually good to go again.

This is a two-for-one meal, as the the chicken and carrots used to make the broth can later be served as a main course. The quality of every ingredient – and in particular the chicken, which should be free-range – is crucial for the success of the dish. Soft, rich egg pasta works very well, and I tend to choose taglierini or tortellini.

In a deep, tall pan, heat up 1 tablespoon of olive oil over a medium heat and add the onion, carrots, celery and passata. Place the chicken drumsticks (or legs) in the pan. Add about 2 litres of cold water, cover with a lid and bring to the boil, then take the lid off, add the half stock cube and season with sea salt. Reduce the heat and simmer for about 45–50 minutes, so that some of the liquid evaporates, concentrating the flavour of the broth.

Meanwhile, bring a saucepan of salted water to the boil and cook the pasta until *al dente* (check the packet and start testing towards the end of the suggested cooking time), then drain.

Divide the pasta between 4 shallow bowls and ladle the hot chicken broth over it, with the celery removed if you prefer. Dust Parmesan on top and serve.

Mamma says

Any remaining broth can be used the following day with a fresh batch of pasta or, alternatively, croutons.

In kitchen folklore, chicken soup is reputed to make you live longer and by cooking all the raw ingredients in cold water without sautéing the onion first, it's even healthier – which will make your GP very happy.

Fish soup

Zuppa di pesce

Serves: 4
Prep: 5 mins
Cooking: 30 mins

Zuppa di pesce is a typically versatile Puglian dish that varies from one area to another. It can be prepared in a dozen different ways – the one unvarying ingredient is monkfish tail. In this recipe I also use langoustines, as they are delicious and the shells help flavour the soup. It can be served with pasta, croutons or toasted bread, and because of its mild flavour it's loved by children of all ages.

Olive oil
1 garlic clove, chopped
3 sprigs of flat parsley
  leaves, chopped
400g cherry tomatoes,
  halved
10 shell-on langoustines
1 monkfish tail
  (about 380g)
Sea salt
Chilli flakes (optional)

Pour 1 tablespoon of olive oil into a deep, tall pan and add the garlic, parsley and cherry tomatoes. Pour in abundant water (enough to cover the fish once you place it in the pan). Bring to the boil with the lid on and then turn down the heat and leave to simmer for another 5 minutes or so.

At this point, place the langoustines and the monkfish in the pan. Add more hot water to cover, if necessary. Sprinkle on some sea salt and, if you like, a pinch of chilli flakes – not too much. Simmer for about 25 minutes, or until the monkfish is cooked through. Taste and adjust the seasoning if necessary.

You can leave the langoustines whole, or take them out of their shells. In that case, remove and shell the langoustines, then roughly chop up the flesh and add it back to the soup.

Next, remove the monkfish. Cut it into chunks and put it back into the soup.

Serve the soup hot with croutons, toasted bread or small pasta such as stelline or farfalline (which should be cooked separately).

Mamma says

You can add more seafood or fish such as halibut, haddock, snapper or red mullet to the soup. Note that the langoustines and monkfish would have to go in the pan before, say, clams or mussels, as they require a longer cooking time. If adding extra ingredients, remember to use a large pan so everything can cook properly.

Vegetables

Neither my children nor I ever need any prodding or coaxing to eat vegetables, luckily. On the contrary, we are all avid eaters of greens and fruit; perhaps it's in the blood, or perhaps it's because in our Puglian cuisine we even eat vegetables at the end of a meal. I can't remember a family meal that ended without some fennel or radishes – they're a boon for your digestion.

Most of the time, Puglian mammas also cook vegetables as a main course with the optional addition, at times, of a small quantity of meat (pancetta, ham or sausage). Vegetables are either eaten raw, dressed with a drizzle of good olive oil, or cooked in a *tiella* – an earthenware pot – and are generally accompanied by rice.

Our streets teem with local producers' pushcarts selling fruit and vegetables, often from small market gardens, and every one of our markets has a dizzying display of fresh crops. I still remember one of my first expeditions to our local market, when I discovered the *vembasciauele*, the wild baby red onions that are so common in our region. I must admit I wasn't crazy about them when I was a child because of their sharp, bitter taste, but every true-born Pugliese adores them and eats them sautéed, boiled or preserved in olive oil. They are considered good for your stomach, as they help digestion, and (I'll whisper this) are rumoured to be an excellent aphrodisiac.

I recommend you also take your children to a local market or, even better, a farm. It's fun for them to pick whichever fruit and vegetables they like directly from the fields – and it's certainly a memorable experience, showing them where their food comes from and helping foster an enduring interest in what they eat.

Green bean salad

Insalata di verdure

Serves: 4
Prep & cooking:
30 mins

A typical vegetable dish of the Bari area is the *insalata mista saporita*, or 'tasty mixed salad', made of ingredients such as lettuce, rocket, young spinach leaves, cucumber, tomatoes, carrots, olives, chives and anchovies, and dressed with vinegar, olive oil, salt and pepper. Tasty it certainly is, but it's also quite strongly flavoured and heavy, and therefore not really suitable for children.

My green salad is a much lighter version of the original Barese recipe, and I have used it many times for packed lunches. If you are planning to do the same, just bear in mind that you will have to make it in the morning, because if you do it the previous evening then it will lose all its freshness and crunchiness overnight.

That means you may have to wake up ten minutes earlier than usual. But before you busy yourself in the kitchen, make sure you're totally awake and not half asleep as I was once, when I put two eggs straight from the fridge into boiling water. The resulting explosion transformed them into a piece of conceptual art. That day Emiliano and Eleonora had a sandwich in their packed lunch.

3 firm-textured
 potatoes (such as
 Charlotte)
200g fine green beans,
 topped, tailed and
 halved
1 cucumber
3 medium tomatoes
1 tin of tuna in olive
 oil, drained
Olive oil
Sea salt

In separate pans, boil the potatoes (about 20 minutes) and the green beans (about 10 minutes).

Meanwhile, peel and chop the cucumber, and chop the tomatoes. Put them in a salad bowl, along with the tuna. Drain the green beans and add them to the bowl. Drizzle on 1 tablespoon of olive oil.

When the potatoes are cooked, drain and leave to cool for a few minutes, then peel, chop and mix into the salad. Season with salt.

Let the salad rest for a few minutes, then serve.

Mamma says

If your child is not a great fan of tuna, you can simply replace it with 1 or 2 chopped up hard-boiled eggs. The fresher the eggs, the harder they are to peel, so if you don't want to lose your temper and composure, use eggs that have been in the fridge for at least a week.

Potato salad with shallots

Patate all'agro

Serves: 4
Prep: 5 mins
Cooking: 20–25 mins

Potatoes and shallots (or spring onions) form a tasty combination, and what I particularly like about *patate all'agro* is the freshness and fragrance that come from the raw ingredients and sour dressing. This means that the salad also works very well as a side dish for fish.

I once prepared a large bowl of *patate all'agro* for a literary picnic to which we had been invited. Ten minutes after placing the bowl on the table, it was scraped clean – evidently the potato salad was much more interesting than the author's talk.

700g firm-textured potatoes (such as Charlotte)
1 shallot or spring onion (white part), finely sliced
3 sprigs of flat parsley leaves, finely chopped
1 tbsp white wine vinegar
Olive oil
Fine salt

Bring the potatoes to the boil in a large pan of water, then turn down the heat and simmer for about 20–25 minutes until they are tender. Drain in a colander and leave until cool enough to handle.

Remove the skins and chop the potatoes into chunks. Place in a salad bowl and add the the sliced shallot (or spring onion), chopped parsley and the white wine vinegar, 3 tablespoons of olive oil and 1 teaspoon of fine salt, then mix all the ingredients until they are well amalgamated. Serve warm or cold.

Mamma says

Boiling the potatoes with their skin on makes them easy to peel and retains more flavour – you can check that they are properly cooked by piercing them with a cocktail stick.

If you don't have a shallot or spring onion to hand, you can use the tender heart of a small onion. But go easy with the quantity, or it can overwhelm the other ingredients. For extra flavour, you could also add capers and black olives.

Mushrooms with pancetta

Funghi con pancetta

Serves: 4
Prep & cooking:
20 mins

Some children are suspicious of mushrooms. Ours started by eating them together with pasta, and I recommend you use the same ruse: it's the perfect introduction to this flavourful food, full of important nutrients and the perfect vegetarian substitute for meat.

This is another versatile recipe that works very well both as a side dish or as a main, if served with tagliatelle or pappardelle pasta. Mixing different kinds of mushrooms yields the best result. My favourite combination is the soft-textured and delicately flavoured oyster mushrooms, the slightly fruity enoki mushrooms and the stronger-tasting chestnut mushrooms, which are ideal for pasta dishes. If you happen to find fresh porcini, then I suggest you use them on their own, as their flavour is so unique that it would be a shame to mix them with other mushrooms.

150g oyster
  mushrooms
100g enoki
  mushrooms
200g chestnut
  mushrooms
Olive oil
1 garlic clove, finely
  chopped
Fine salt
10 cherry tomatoes,
  halved
3 sprigs of flat parsley
  leaves, chopped
100g pancetta cubes
1 tbsp grated Pecorino
  Romano

First, clean the mushrooms. Make sure they are thoroughly and quickly washed and dried. Don't leave them under running water for too long as they might get soggy. Slice the smaller mushrooms and chop the larger mushrooms into pieces that are roughly the same thickness.

Heat up 1 tablespoon of olive oil in a saucepan and in it sauté the chopped garlic clove. Add the mushrooms, along with a pinch of salt, and leave to cook for 2–3 minutes, until they exude all their moisture.

Next, add the halved cherry tomatoes, chopped parsley, pancetta and Pecorino. Cook for about 15 minutes, stirring from time to time, then remove from the heat. Serve hot or cold.

Mamma says

If you prefer a meat-free dish, don't add the pancetta cubes. In that case, you can give the dish extra flavour by adding a third of a vegetable stock cube to the saucepan with the other ingredients.

Peas with pancetta

Piselli con pancetta

Serves: 4
Prep: 5 mins
Cooking: 15 mins

If your children are reluctant to eat peas, this is the recipe to convert them. It is an excellent side dish that goes very well with fish, although my mamma serves it as a main course with rice.

You can use fresh peas instead of frozen, if you like. Shelling the pods can be quite a laborious affair, but it's something that children love doing (I always did – sneaking one or two peas into my mouth now and then).

Olive oil
1 shallot, chopped
50g small pancetta
  cubes (about 1cm)
400g frozen petits pois
Sea salt

Heat up 1 tablespoon of olive oil in a shallow pan on a medium heat, then add the shallot and the pancetta cubes. Leave to sizzle for a few minutes, stirring occasionally, until the pancetta sweats its fat and changes colour but hasn't yet turned brown.

Add the peas and a pinch of salt. Stir and then pour 50ml of hot water from the kettle into the pan. Cover the pan partially with a lid and cook on a low heat for about 10–15 minutes, until the water is totally absorbed and the peas are tender. Serve hot or wait until the peas cool down a bit.

Mamma says

If you are using fresh shelled peas, the cooking time will be longer (about 15–20 minutes, adding a little more hot water if necessary).

If you decide to serve the peas with rice, I recommend you cook it separately. Any leftover peas can be stored in the fridge and then mixed with plain boiled rice to create an excellent salad.

Deep-fried vegetables
Frittelle di verdure

Serves: 4
Prep: 20–30 mins
Cooking: 15–20 mins

This is one of those dishes you can improvise at the drop of a hat. Even if you don't have all the ingredients, you can just use any vegetables you can unearth in your fridge – and because they are so tasty, *frittelle* are the perfect way to introduce children to more 'problematic' vegetables such as broccoli and artichokes.

Although they are a bit messy, *frittelle* are incredibly simple to make. Depending on how greedy you are on the day, you can serve them as an appetiser, as a side or even as a main course.

250g firm-textured
  potatoes (such
  as Charlotte)
3 small Italian or
  French artichokes,
  or 1 globe artichoke
Juice of ½ lemon or
  1 tbsp white wine
  vinegar
3 courgettes (about
  250g)
4 courgette flowers
  (if available)
¼ x mozzarella
  (40g), diced
2 anchovies, washed
  and halved

For the batter
About 100g '00' white
  flour
Fine salt
Sunflower oil, for
  deep-frying

Peel and cut the potatoes into slices about 1mm thick.

Cut the artichokes' stems off, then peel off the outer, harder leaves until you get to the tender leaves inside. Be extra careful if they are thorny. Trim off any small leaves from the base and chop off about 4cm from the top of the artichokes – discard the trimmings and all the leaves.

Cut the artichokes into vertical slices, about 2–3mm thick (if you're using a globe artichoke instead of the small ones, make sure you remove all of the furry choke before slicing). Place the slices in a bowl and cover with hot water from the kettle, adding the lemon or vinegar. This will soften them and take the bitterness away, as well as preventing discolouration. Leave in the bowl for about 3 minutes, then drain and set aside.

Wash the courgettes and slice them into rounds about 2–3mm thick.

Wash the courgette flowers and dry them, then stick a mozzarella cube and half an anchovy into each one. Twist the top of the courgette flowers closed, to avoid spillage while they're frying.

Now that the vegetables are all ready, prepare the batter. Tip the flour into a bowl. Use a fork to mix in enough water to create a creamy mixture – about 200ml. Sprinkle in some fine salt. This should make enough batter. If you need more, it's quick enough to make extra, using the same 1:2 ratio of flour:water.

Meanwhile, pour enough sunflower oil into a deep pan to fill it by no more than a third. Heat to a frying temperature of 180°C (or when a cube of bread turns golden-brown in a minute); if it is too hot, turn down the heat slightly. One by one, roll 7 or 8 potato slices in the batter. Carefully lower them into the hot oil and fry until they turn a light golden colour. Remove the battered potato slices from the pan with a slotted spoon and leave them to dry in a bowl lined with kitchen paper.

Following the same procedure, fry the remaining potato slices, then the courgettes, then the courgette flowers and finally the artichokes. It is important to fry the vegetables in small batches to avoid sticking; allow the oil to re-heat between batches.

Sprinkle fine salt on the fried vegetables and serve. In my family, we tend to eat the *frittelle* straight away, as they are tastier when piping hot.

Mamma says

For the artichokes, you could also make the traditional batter using 100g flour, 1 egg yolk, 1 tablespoon of freshly grated Parmesan, water and salt.

If you want to use broccoli or cauliflower for *frittelle*, boil them whole for 3 or 5 minutes respectively before draining them, then cut into slices 3–4mm thick. Roll them in batter and fry.

Roasted peppers

Peperoni arrostiti

Serves: 4
Prep: 5 mins
Cooking: 25 mins (plus
  marinating time)

In Puglia, we prepare peppers in many different ways, and they are fantastic both as an *antipasto* and as a side dish to accompany meat or cheese. My grandmother always had several jars of peppers preserved in olive oil in her kitchen. She kept them hidden away on the higher shelves, out of the reach of small curious hands. Roasting is just one way of cooking this delicious vegetable – and it only takes five minutes of preparation. The roasted peppers taste even better after being left for a day.

4 yellow peppers
  (or a mix of red,
  orange and yellow)
3 sprigs of flat parsley
  leaves, chopped
1½ garlic cloves,
  finely chopped
Olive oil
Fine salt

Preheat the oven to 220°C/Gas 7 and line a baking tray with foil.

Wash and dry the peppers. Place them on the lined tray, and then roast them in the oven for about 25 minutes, turning frequently.

The peppers are ready when the skin blisters and starts turning dark brown, and the flesh feels tender when prodded with a fork, but the peppers haven't collapsed. Remove the tray from the oven and leave the peppers until cool enough to handle.

Slit the peppers and drain off any excess moisture. Take the skin off and remove the seeds inside, then cut the pepper flesh into thin strips and place on a flat dish. Add the parsley and garlic, and season with olive oil and salt. Mix well, cover the dish and leave to marinate for 10 minutes or more before serving.

Serve with a slice of Altamura bread (see page 155) or a sliver of *provolone piccante* – or any other crusty bread or strong cheese.

Mamma says

There are lots of other ways to prepare peppers. In our family we often cut them into thin strips and pan-fry them with garlic, onion, chopped tomatoes, parsley, salt and freshly ground black pepper. Or they can be sweated in oil, vinegar and sugar; or roasted and seasoned with parsley and capers.

Oven-baked fennel

Finocchi gratinati

Serves: 4
Prep: 10 mins
Cooking: 25 mins

Fennel is a common ingredient in Puglia, and can be eaten as a main, as a side dish or even to refresh the palate at the end of a rich meal. Fennel seeds are ideal for digestive drinks, especially during winter. (A simple fennel infusion without any added sugar or honey can be given to babies to reduce gas in their little bellies.)

My children and I love fennel, and I often serve it *pinzimonio*-style, which means raw with just a little bit of olive oil, salt and pepper. But my favourite fennel recipe is this gratin – one of the simplest recipes in my repertoire – which is delicious and full of Mediterranean flavour.

Olive oil
4 fennel bulbs
Fine salt
4 tbsp milk
50g soft white
  breadcrumbs

Preheat the oven to 180°C/Gas 4 and grease a ceramic baking dish with olive oil.

Wash the fennel bulbs under cold water, then cut off and discard the stalks. Remove the external hard leaves and then cut each bulb lengthwise into thick slices.

Boil the fennel slices in salted water for about 5 minutes. Drain and place in the greased baking dish.

Pour on the milk and sprinkle over the breadcrumbs. Drizzle over some olive oil and season with salt. Put the baking dish in the oven for about 25 minutes, until the breadcrumbs turn golden-brown. Serve hot or cold.

Mamma says

Make sure you buy fresh fennel. Look at the crispness of the outer leaves and, most importantly, the colour of the base, which should be white and not discoloured.

Southern Italian purists, look away now. For this recipe, you can use butter rather than olive oil to grease the baking dish.

Accompanied by crackers and cheese, this makes an ideal packed lunch.

Golden baked cabbage

Cavolo al forno

Serves: 4
Prep: 5 mins
Cooking: 15–20 mins

Since it contains antioxidants and important nutrients, white cabbage ranks among the healthiest vegetables around. It goes without saying that eating it would do your kids a world of good.

The trouble is that children are not especially keen on cabbage in general, and white cabbage in particular. This recipe, however, may change their attitude and show them that healthy food doesn't have to taste bad, smell even worse and look unappetising. A golden baked cabbage is easy to make and can be served as a side or a main.

2 knobs (about 15–20g) of unsalted butter, plus extra for greasing
1 white cabbage
Fine salt
100g small pancetta cubes (about 1cm)
Olive oil
2 tbsp breadcrumbs

Preheat the oven to 180°C/Gas 4 and grease a ceramic baking dish with butter.

Wash the white cabbage under running water. Quarter it with a knife and discard the core and the base. Cut into slices and blanch in slightly salted boiling water for about 5 minutes.

Drain the cabbage thoroughly and place in the greased dish. Scatter over the pancetta cubes and sprinkle on some salt (not too much, as pancetta is already salty). Drizzle over a little olive oil and scatter the breadcrumbs on top.

Put the dish in the oven for about 15–20 minutes, or until the cabbage turns golden-brown. Serve hot.

Mamma says

For a non-meat version, you can replace the pancetta cubes with a dusting of freshly grated Pecorino.

If you have older children, why not try baked cauliflower or broccoli? Just boil in slightly salted water for about 15 minutes, then cut into florets and dry. Place the florets in a ceramic baking dish greased with butter or olive oil.

Dust the florets with Parmesan, sprinkle on some salt and bake in the oven for about 20 minutes, until tender but crisp.

Around 5 minutes before the florets are cooked, lay a couple of slices of mild cheese over the top to melt.

Courgette parmigiana

Parmigiana di zucchine

Serves: 4
Prep: 40 mins
Cooking: 20 mins

Known in Molfettese dialect as *parmeggéne*, this traditional Italian dish has travelled across the world, heralded by generation after generation of emigrants from the *Bel Paese* ('beautiful country'). My mamma's cousin, who has been living in New Jersey since the age of three, still cooks it religiously as her own mother used to do it, with layers of pan-fried aubergines covered by tomato sauce.

My *parmigiana* is lighter than the original version and I use courgettes rather than aubergines, as children seem to prefer the sweeter taste. It can be served as a side dish or as a main – it also works perfectly for a packed lunch. The only problem is that it takes a little while to prepare, so it's better to make it the night before.

1kg courgettes
Fine salt
2 eggs
50g '00' white flour
Olive oil
Parmesan
2 x mozzarelle (250g),
  diced

For the tomato sauce
Olive oil
½ onion, finely sliced
500ml passata
1 x 400g tin plum
  tomatoes
1 celery stalk, roughly
  chopped
1 carrot, roughly
  chopped
3 sprigs of flat parsley
  leaves, roughly
  chopped
Sea salt

Cut off the ends of the courgettes and slice them lengthways, about 2–3mm thick. Place the slices on a dish and sprinkle over a little salt. Leave for about 30 minutes, so that the courgettes can release some of their water. To squeeze out any excess moisture from the courgettes, my mamma puts a weight on top of them, which can be something pretty primitive such as a mug or a tin of tomatoes.

To make the tomato sauce, heat up 1 tablespoon of olive oil in a saucepan on a medium heat. Sizzle the onion in the pan until it is translucent, then pour in the passata and tinned tomatoes. Add the celery, carrot and parsley, and a pinch of salt. Pour in 150ml water, cover with a lid and bring to the boil, then turn down the heat and let simmer for 20 minutes. Season with more salt, to taste.

Meanwhile, prepare the courgettes. First dab off any excess water with a clean tea towel or kitchen paper (or else your hob, your shirt and your entire kitchen will end up being splattered with olive oil).

Beat the eggs in one shallow bowl and put the flour in another. Pour 3 tablespoons of olive oil into a non-stick frying pan and heat to a high temperature. One by one, dip a few courgette slices in the beaten egg and coat with the flour before frying first one side then the other to golden-brown. Transfer the fried slices to a plate lined with kitchen paper. Repeat with the rest of the slices.

Preheat the oven to 200°C/Gas 6. Once the tomato sauce is ready, use it to cover the bottom of a ceramic baking dish (about 30 x 20cm). Lay the courgette slices over the top and scatter on some freshly grated Parmesan.

Cover the courgettes with more tomato sauce and scatter over some mozzarella cubes. Form more layers following the same procedure until you have used all the courgette slices and mozzarella. Finish the top layer with an abundant quantity of tomato sauce, a generous dusting of Parmesan and a sprinkling of salt.

Place the tray in the preheated oven for about 15–20 minutes, until the cheesy top is patched with brown. Allow the *parmigiana* to cool down a little before serving.

Potatoes with a scent of runaway lamb

Patate all'agnello scappato

Serves: 4
Prep: 5 mins
Cooking: 25–30 mins

In this dish, the potatoes are there, but the lamb – well, the lamb has 'run away'. It's a very old recipe, hailing from the time when meat was a luxury not everyone could afford. The mere mention of the word 'lamb' and the combination of herbs (also used to season real lamb dishes) gave people who couldn't afford meat the impression of eating it.

Potatoes with a scent of runaway lamb are a perfect side for any meat dish. They deceive my family's palates each time; Emiliano will inevitably cry, 'Where's the lamb gone?' whilst looking for it under the table.

Olive oil
700g potatoes
  (any type), peeled
  and chopped into
  3–4cm dice
½ glass of white wine
  (about 75ml)
4–5 bay leaves
1 sprig of rosemary
4–5 sage leaves
1 garlic clove, peeled
1–2 tsp sea salt
Black pepper

Preheat the oven to 180°C/Gas 4 and grease a roasting tray with olive oil.

Place the diced potatoes on the greased roasting tray, then add the half-glass of wine and the same quantity of water. Add the bay leaves, rosemary, sage leaves and garlic, and season with sea salt, to taste. Drizzle over a little olive oil and grind on some black pepper.

Place the tray in the oven for about 30 minutes, until the potatoes are cooked and all the liquid has evaporated. Serve hot.

Mamma says

Don't worry about using wine in a dish for children, since most of the alcohol boils away during cooking.

Minestrone vegetables

Minestrone secco

Serves: 4–6
Prep: 15 mins (plus
   pre-soaking the rice)
Cooking: 40 mins

The word *minestrone* means a soup made out of seasonal vegetables – a good way of using up extra vegetables that will otherwise go to waste.

The *minestrone* below is dry, however, cooked *tiella*-style with the ingredients layered up in a pot. My aunt first recommended it to me, and the result exceeded all expectations.

200g Arborio or other
   risotto rice
Olive oil
½ onion, sliced
500g potatoes (any
   type), peeled and cut
   into 2mm slices
1 aubergine, cut into
   1–2cm slices
1 yellow pepper, cut
   into thin strips
1 carrot, sliced
1 courgette, sliced
400g cherry tomatoes,
   halved
1–1½ tbsp grated
   Parmesan
Sea salt

Soak the rice in cold water for 20–30 minutes to make it tender. Preheat the oven to 180°C/Gas 4.

Grease the base of a ceramic baking dish or an earthenware pot (around 24–28cm across) with 2–3 tablespoons of olive oil. Scatter in half the onion slices, then pack in half the potato slices. Add more layers, distributing loosely: half of the aubergine slices, then half of the yellow pepper strips, half of the carrot slices, and then half of the courgette slices.

Drain the rice and spread it on top of the vegetables (don't worry if a little bit of water ends up in the dish). Cover the rice with the tomatoes, facing cut-side down. Dust on the Parmesan and a pinch of sea salt.

Layer on the remaining ingredients in reverse order: courgette, carrot, yellow pepper, aubergine, potato, then onion. Drizzle a tablespoon of olive oil on top. Pour on a glass of water (150ml).

Put the dish in the oven for 40 minutes. The *minestrone* is ready when the rice is cooked and the vegetables are tender.

Mamma says

I think I can hear someone say: 'Hang on – what kind of *dry* minestrone is it if you are adding a glass of water at the end?' All right, so it isn't completely dry. But busy mums have no time for pedants – what's important to them is that a dish tastes delicious. Other veg ideas are broccoli, cauliflower and butternut squash.

Stuffed peppers

Peperoni ripieni

Serves: 4
Prep: 10 mins
Cooking: 30–40 mins

One day, my mamma's oven broke down and she asked me to go to take our earthenware *tiella* pot to a public wood-fired oven. I thought that such ovens were just a thing of the past – but I was wrong. From two streets away, I was engulfed by a fabulous mixture of fragrances: oven-baked pasta mingling with focaccia in the air. I handed my precious earthenware pot to the owner, who was wearing a white vest drenched in sweat and listening to the latest cheesy hit on his transistor radio.

The oven's temperature must have been close to that of the surface of the sun, and I felt as if my hands, feet and nose were beginning to melt. My pot contained vegetarian stuffed peppers – other women had meaty versions, with minced meat, anchovies or pancetta cubes. Interesting though this comparison was, I must admit I was rather glad when the sweaty man handed me a slip of paper with my name on it and I could step outside to wait.

Olive oil
4 yellow peppers
2 eggs
1 tbsp grated Parmesan or Pecorino Romano
2 x mozzarelle (250g), diced
1 tbsp capers
Leaves from 3 sprigs of flat parsley, chopped
Sea salt
8 cherry tomatoes, halved
2 tbsp breadcrumbs

Preheat the oven to 180°C/Gas 4. Grease the bottom of a ceramic baking dish (about 30 x 20cm) with about ½ tablespoon of olive oil.

Cut around the stalks of the peppers and pull them out, then cut the peppers in half lengthways and remove the seeds. Alternatively, you can leave the stalks in.

Snugly position the pepper halves in the dish, in a single layer.

Use a fork to mix together the eggs in a bowl and add half the Parmesan (or Pecorino). Mix in the mozzarella, capers, parsley, some salt and a drizzle of olive oil.

Spoon the mixture into the pepper halves. Divide the tomato halves between the stuffed peppers, cut-side up. Dust with the rest of the Parmesan and the breadcrumbs, and drizzle on a bit more olive oil.

Place the dish in the preheated oven for about 30–40 minutes. Use a fork or a cocktail stick to see if the peppers are properly cooked. Leave to cool before serving.

Mamma says

For added effect, you can cook whole peppers without cutting them
in half, as my mamma does. For this 'monumental' version of the
dish, use big yellow peppers with a fairly flat base, as they need to
stand in the baking tray.

Slice off the tops of the peppers and put them to one side.

Remove the seeds from inside the peppers, then wash the peppers
and place them upside-down to dry.

Prepare filling as opposite, then stuff the peppers. Use the
reserved pepper tops as lids, and secure them firmly with cocktail
sticks (to be removed before serving). To avoid any spillage, make
sure that you don't fill the peppers to the brim before putting on
the lids. Cook in the oven as usual, and then serve.

Stuffed aubergines

Melanzane ripiene

Serves: 4–6
Prep: 20 mins
Cooking: 40 mins

This recipe is known in my town as *cap de muerte* because of the aubergine's resemblance to a dead man's head, a fact that horrifies and thrills children in equal measure. A very similar dish can be found in Spanish restaurants – perhaps this is not too much of a surprise, since Puglia was under Spanish rule for quite a long time.

3 aubergines
1 tbsp white wine
   (or cider) vinegar
1 tsp sea salt
Olive oil
1 garlic clove, chopped
2 eggs
2 tbsp breadcrumbs
2 tbsp grated Pecorino
   Romano
3 sprigs of flat parsley
   leaves, chopped
Fresh oregano, for
   garnishing (optional)

For the tomato sauce
Olive oil
1 garlic clove, chopped
200g tinned plum
   tomatoes
2 basil leaves, roughly
   chopped
Sea salt

First prepare the tomato sauce. Heat up 1 tablespoon of olive oil in a saucepan over a medium heat and sauté the garlic. Add the tinned tomatoes, the basil, a pinch of salt and 100ml water. Cook for about 20 minutes, stirring occasionally, so the sauce is partially reduced.

Meanwhile, chop the stems off the aubergines and cut in half lengthwise. Fill a large cooking pot with water and bring it to the boil. Add the vinegar and the teaspoon of salt. Place the aubergines inside and boil for about 5 minutes. Drain and leave to cool.

With a spoon, scoop out the soft pulp from the aubergines, leaving an outer shell about 1cm thick. Dice the pulp into cubes, squeezing out any excess water.

Preheat the oven to 180°C/Gas 4, and line a ceramic dish (about 30 x 20cm) with baking parchment.

Next make the filling. Heat 1 tablespoon of olive oil in a frying pan over a medium heat and sauté the garlic. Add the aubergine cubes and cook for about 3-4 minutes, then set aside.

Crack and whisk the eggs in a bowl, then mix in the breadcrumbs, Pecorino, parsley and sautéed aubergine cubes.

Now place the scooped-out aubergines in the lined dish. Spoon the filling into the aubergines and cover them with tomato sauce.

Drizzle on some olive oil before putting the dish in the oven for 20 minutes. Leave the aubergines to cool for 10 minutes, and serve warm with a sprinkling of oregano, if you like.

Beef tomatoes stuffed with rice

Pomodori al riso

Serves: 4
Prep: 10 mins
Cooking: 40 mins (plus pre-soaking the rice)

This classic summer dish takes just ten minutes to make in advance. When your guests arrive, just stick it in the oven and, while you're having a chat or a drink with them, observe the effect of its mouth-watering smell on their faces.

You may want to accompany this dish with a good soft cheese to bring all the delicate flavours into focus. My favourite is *sottocenere al tartufo* (or *sottocenere tartufato*), which is made with truffles and aged in an ash rind, but any well-flavoured cheese works well.

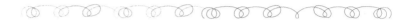

7 tbsp Arborio or other risotto rice (about 100g)
4 beef tomatoes
1 garlic clove
5–10 basil leaves, depending on size, plus optional extra for garnishing
Olive oil
Sea salt

Soak the rice in cold water for 20–30 minutes to make it tender. Preheat the oven to 180°C/Gas 4.

Slice the tomatoes close to the top, creating a lid 4–5 mm thick. Hollow out each tomato, scooping out the pulp with a teaspoon or a knife without damaging the walls. Place it in a bowl, removing the harder bits. Finely chop the garlic and basil, then mix them in.

Boil the rice in a pan of salted water for 5 minutes, or 8 minutes if you like well-done rice, and drain it. Mix into the tomato mixture.

Nearly fill each tomato with 2 tablespoons of mixture. Place the lids on top, pinning with cocktail sticks if necessary.

Grease the bottom of a roasting tray with a dash of olive oil and place the four tomatoes inside, kissing like billiard balls.

Sprinkle a little bit of olive oil and a pinch of salt on the tomatoes' lids. Cook in the oven for 35 minutes, or until the lids turn brown. Before serving the tomatoes, leave them in the oven for a few minutes to rest. Garnish with basil leaves, if you like, and serve.

Mamma says

For bonus potato wedges, peel some potatoes and cut them into wedges. Add olive oil, salt and rosemary. Bake the wedges for 5–10 minutes, then place the stuffed tomatoes on the tray and cook as above.

Salento potato pie

Pitta salentina

Serves: 4
Prep: 10 mins (plus potato cooking time)
Cooking: 40 mins

This stuffed potato cake is a traditional peasant recipe and a perfect example of rural Puglian cuisine at its best, creating complex flavours from only a few ingredients.

1kg floury or all-purpose potatoes (such as King Edward or Maris Piper)
Olive oil
1 garlic clove, peeled
3 medium onions, finely sliced
2–3 anchovies, drained of oil, or washed and desalted
2 tbsp pitted black olives, roughly chopped
½ courgette, chopped into slices up to 3mm thick
2 basil leaves, finely chopped
6 mint leaves, finely chopped
1 tbsp capers
3 tbsp passata
100g grated Pecorino Romano
50g grated Parmesan
2 eggs
3 sprigs of flat parsley leaves
50g breadcrumbs

Preheat the oven to 200°C/Gas 6.

Boil the unpeeled potatoes in abundant water, until tender. Drain and allow to cool enough to be handled.

Meanwhile, heat 2 tablespoons of olive oil in a frying pan over a medium-low heat. Add the garlic and onions. Sweat for a minute or two, then add about 30ml water. Add the anchovies, along with the olives, courgette, basil and half of the mint, then mix. Add a little more water to the pan, then stir and carry on cooking.

After about 5 minutes, add the capers and the passata. Pour in a little bit more water and cover the pan with a lid. Leave to simmer for 10–12 minutes more on a low heat, stirring now and then, until the sauce becomes thickish but not sloppy. Add some more water if necessary and don't let all the liquid evaporate.

Peel the cooked potatoes and mash them one by one with the prongs of a fork (this way they won't release too much starch).

Place the mashed potatoes in a bowl and add half of the Pecorino and half of the Parmesan. Crack the eggs and add them to the bowl, along with the parsley, remaining mint, half of the breadcrumbs and 2 tablespoons of olive oil.

Mix all the ingredients gently with your hands until you get a smooth and pliable mixture. If it's too dry, add a little bit of water or milk. Make sure you don't mix for too long, otherwise starch will be released by the potatoes and the mixture will take on a gluey, purée-like texture.

Continues overleaf

Now pour 3 tablespoons of olive oil into a ceramic baking dish (30 x 20cm). With your hands, spread the olive oil over the base and along the sides.

Fill a bowl with cold tap water to wet your hands with, so that the potato mixture won't stick to them. Split the potato mixture into two parts, one slightly bigger than the other. From the larger part, take some mixture and cover the base of the tray little by little, forming a layer about 1cm thick. Wet your hands each time you're about to handle more mixture.

At this point, take the lid off the pan and remove the garlic clove from the sauce. Pour the sauce over the potato layer, spreading it evenly with a spoon. Dust over the remaining cheese. Wet your hands and, using the rest of the potato mixture, form the top layer.

Drizzle some olive oil and splash a bit of water over the top of the potato pie, spreading it evenly with your wet hands to create a moist, creamy top. Finally, scatter on the rest of the breadcrumbs.

Put the tray in the oven for about 35–40 minutes, until the breadcrumbs turn golden-brown. Leave to cool before serving.

Mamma says

Chopping onions may be a very moving experience, but you can hold back tears simply by wetting your wrists or soaking the onions in water before slicing them.

If you and your children like a bit of heat, throw in some chilli flakes when you add the capers and the passata.

This is one of the things that tastes even better the day after you've cooked it. It is not difficult to prepare, but it requires a longish preparation time, so I suggest you make it at the weekend, preferably when your neighbours are away – or you may find them sniffing around outside your front door.

Potato cake

Pizza di patate

Serves: 4
Prep: 15 mins
Cooking: 20 mins

Every time I go back to Puglia to visit my parents, I know that my mamma will welcome me with a freshly baked slice of *pizza di patate*. I regard this as the chief of all Puglian recipes. It's very light and can be served as a starter, a main or a side – and it can be eaten hot or cold.

All my friends love potato cake too, and among ourselves we call it *salva cena*, 'emergency meal'. It is so easy to prepare that you could even delegate it to your couch-potato husband while you sip a well-deserved glass of wine after a long day at work.

1kg floury or all-purpose potatoes (such as Estima or King Edward)
100ml milk
1½ tbsp olive oil
1 egg
Fine salt
1 tbsp grated Parmesan
6 tbsp breadcrumbs
1 x mozzarella (125g), diced
50g small pancetta cubes (about 1cm) or shredded slices of Italian cooked ham

Boil the unpeeled potatoes in abundant water, until tender. Drain and allow to cool enough for handling.

Peel the cooked potatoes and mash them with the prongs of a fork. Add the milk, the olive oil and the egg. Stir to create a smooth and creamy mixture. Stir in ½ teaspoon of salt and the Parmesan.

Preheat the oven to 180°C/Gas 4, then scatter half of the breadcrumbs over the base of a ceramic baking dish (about 30 x 20cm).

Spread half of the potato mixture into the tray, using a spoon to create an even layer around 2cm thick. Scatter over the mozzarella and pancetta cubes (or shredded ham).

Add another layer of the potato mixture on top. Drizzle on some olive oil and splash on a little water – spread evenly with wetted hands to create a creamy and moist top. Finally, scatter over the rest of the breadcrumbs.

Put the dish in the oven for 15–20 minutes, until the breadcrumbs go brown. Cut into slices and serve hot or cold.

Artichokes baked with potatoes and rice

Carciofi, patate e riso

Serves: 4
Prep: 15 mins (plus pre-soaking the rice)
Cooking: 35–40 mins

I created this recipe when one of our son's friends was over for a play date. I'd heard his mother complain before about his fickle appetite, and as she dropped him off she'd said,'Don't worry if he doesn't eat: he's a bit fussy. I'll give him a sandwich later.' I gave her child a good long look – the bony knees, the bloodless face, the dark rings under his eyes. 'Leave it with me,' I thought.

I decided to adapt a well-known Puglian recipe called *riso, patate e cozze* (rice, potatoes and mussels), and this was the result. Well, the little boy followed Emiliano's example and ate two whole portions – he hardly paused for breath.

200g Arborio or other risotto rice
4 small Italian or French artichokes (or 160g prepared chargrilled artichokes)
A little lemon juice or a dash of white wine vinegar
Sea salt
1 onion, finely sliced
3 sprigs of flat parsley leaves, roughly chopped
1 garlic clove, finely chopped
Olive oil
400g cherry tomatoes, halved
600g potatoes (any type), peeled and cut into 2cm slices
2 tbsp grated Pecorino Romano
60g breadcrumbs
1 shallot, sliced

Soak the rice in cold water for 20–30 minutes to make it tender, then drain. Preheat the oven to 180°C/Gas 4.

Cut the artichokes' stems off, then peel off the outer, harder leaves until you get to the tender leaves inside. Be careful if they are thorny. Trim off any small leaves from the base and chop off 4cm from the top. Place in a bowl with hot water from the kettle, adding the lemon juice or vinegar. This will soften the artichokes and take the bitterness away, as well as preventing discolouration. Leave in the bowl for about 3 minutes, then drain carefully, squeezing out any remaining water. Slice lengthways, about 3–4mm thick.

Boil the soaked rice in a pan of salted water for 5 minutes, and then drain.

Meanwhile, mix together the onion, parsley and garlic in a bowl.

Pour 2 tablespoons of olive oil into a ceramic baking dish (about 30 x 20cm). Place half of the cherry tomatoes in the dish, cut-side up. Spread half of the onion-parsley-garlic mix evenly on top. Layer on the sliced artichokes and half the potato slices, then cover with the parboiled rice. Spread on the rest of the tomatoes and then the remaining onion-parsley-garlic mix. Sprinkle over a pinch of salt, some olive oil and the Pecorino. Finally, layer on the rest of the potato slices.

Sprinkle the breadcrumbs on top, drizzle over a dash of olive oil and add a pinch of sea salt, then scatter on the sliced shallot. Pour over a little water (about 100ml) to help the rice and vegetables to cook.

Put the tray in the preheated oven for 35–40 minutes, or until the potatoes are tender. Serve warm.

Mamma says

If you can't find Italian or French artichokes, use the chargrilled ones sold at the deli counter of supermarkets, or those preserved in olive oil. Make sure you drain them before use and avoid the kind with chilli, as children can be fussy about spicy food.

olio
di
oliva

Fish

Fish was something that I used to eat at least four times a week as a child growing up in Puglia. My father used to tell me: 'Eat it: it will make you brainy.' I always thought that fish had a sort of special power which one day would unleash in me a super-mind capable of penetrating the mysteries of the universe. I am still waiting patiently for my moment.

Fishermen have always fascinated me. Not in that sense. I mean the way they mend their nets, the way they talk about their catch or paint their boats. Once I took part in a local photography competition, and my project was to capture a fisherman's life of hardship and privation through the eye of the camera. Wandering around the silent port at dawn and seeing the fishermen's sleepless, sun-etched faces and their angular bodies surrounded by piles of fish was an incredible experience.

Since Puglia has such an extended and varied coastline – from the rocky shores of the Adriatic to the sandy beaches of the Ionian – it comes as no surprise that the products of the sea dominate our cuisine. The Mediterranean octopus is a particular favourite; in summer, children fish it from the sea with their bare hands using a small stick or a baited piece of wire and then bash it against the rocks to make it tender, eating it raw. My own children also love *polpo*, as it's called in Italian, and they are happy to eat it grilled, boiled or dressed in a tomato sauce.

Some typically Mediterranean fish can be replaced by similar kinds from the Atlantic, if need be. Of course the taste will be slightly different due to the diverse levels of salt present in these two seas, but as long as the fish is fresh and its preparation simple, nothing else matters.

Feeding fish to children is not such a challenge as people may think, if you start them on it from an early age and use recipes that are mild-flavoured but tasty.

Sea bream baked in foil

Orata al cartoccio

Serves: 4
Prep: 5 mins
Cooking: 30 mins

I serve this dish still in its foil wrapping, like a kind of shiny gift for sharing – it's a way of cooking fish that preserves all the moisture and delicate taste. (Obviously, be careful with the bones if you are giving it to babies or toddlers. Once our daughter Eleonora refused to eat fish for two weeks after swallowing a tiny bone; she relented only after a hefty parental contribution to her piggy bank.)

2 sea bream, gutted and scaled but with head and skin on
Olive oil
2 garlic cloves
3 sprigs of flat parsley leaves, chopped
2 tsp capers
Sea salt
2 lemon slices
2 cherry tomatoes, halved
Black pepper (optional)

Preheat the oven to 180°C/Gas 4. Rinse the sea bream under cold water and place them on a plate. Lay out a sheet of foil for each sea bream, big enough to wrap around it. Grease the foil with olive oil and place the fish on top.

Stuff the inside of each sea bream with a garlic clove, a quarter of the parsley, 1 teaspoon of capers, some olive oil and a pinch of salt.

Top each fish with a lemon slice, 2 tomato halves and the rest of the parsley, then sprinkle with more olive oil and salt. Wrap the foil around each fish and fold the edges tightly. Place on a baking tray and bake in the preheated oven for about 30 minutes.

To check that the fish is cooked, slip a knife into the thickest part – the flesh should be opaque right through to the bones. Serve hot, with a good grinding of black pepper, if you like.

Mamma says

You can make your own combination for the stuffing and the seasoning – black olives, sage and thyme all work well.

Estimating the cooking time for fish can be tricky. An old lady once told me to allow 10 minutes for every 2.5cm of thickness of any fish with bones, measured at the fish's thickest point. But I'm bad at maths and I don't think the calculator and the ruler belong in the kitchen. So I suggest you follow her other rule of thumb: if the fish weighs 100g, the cooking time is 17 minutes, if it weighs 200g then 19 minutes, and so on. (In other words, for each extra 100g of weight you should allow 2 more minutes of cooking time.)

Puglian sea bream

Orata alla maniera pugliese

Serves: 4
Prep: 25 mins
Cooking: 20 mins

This dish is a healthy alternative to the sorry-looking fish fingers you can buy in supermarkets, and I guarantee your children will love it. I took inspiration from the original recipe of this name, which involves laying thinly sliced potatoes at the bottom of the baking dish with garlic, parsley and grated Pecorino, placing sea-bream fillets on top and covering with another layer of sliced potatoes seasoned with more Pecorino, some olive oil, salt and pepper. I found, however, that children prefer the version with mashed potatoes, perhaps because the parsley fragments are blended with the potato purée.

I suggest you buy whole fish and ask your fishmonger to do the cleaning, filleting and skinning for you.

5 floury or all-purpose potatoes (such as King Edward or Maris Piper)
1 egg
10g grated Parmesan
3 sprigs of flat parsley leaves, chopped
Fine salt
4 sea bream or sea bass fillets, skinned
Olive oil

Boil the potatoes in abundant water until they are tender. Once they are ready, let them cool slightly before peeling them.

Meanwhile, preheat the oven to 200°C/Gas 6 and line a ceramic baking dish with baking parchment.

Mash the potatoes in a bowl and add the egg, Parmesan and parsley, then season with salt. Mix all the ingredients until you have a smooth purée.

Lay the fish fillets out in the lined baking dish. Spread the purée evenly on top and drizzle over a bit of olive oil. Put the dish in the preheated oven for about 20 minutes, or until the potato layer turns golden-brown. Serve while warm.

Mamma says

If you're tired of using flaccid parsley or having to buy it every other day, you can wash, dry and chop fresh parsley and store it in the fridge in a lidless container for up to a week. It's a little trick one of my Neapolitan friends taught me. (Whenever you need a solution to a practical problem, always ask a Neapolitan!)

Black cod with olives

Merluzzo nero con olive

Serves: 4
Prep: 5 mins
Cooking: 15 mins

Thanks to this delicious recipe, I was able to overcome my aversion to cod – a remnant perhaps of some traumatic experience as a child.

When I cooked black cod for the first time, I was bowled over by its buttery flavour, and since then cod has regained its rightful place in our family's menu – much to the joy of the children and Alessandro. Although the taste will be a little different, you can also use ordinary cod for this dish, so long as it's fresh.

4 black cod fillets,
 skin on
Olive oil
A squeeze of lemon
 juice
1 garlic clove, finely
 chopped
3 sprigs of flat parsley
 leaves, chopped
Fine salt
4 tbsp pitted black
 olives, chopped

Wash the fish fillets under running water and dry them with kitchen paper.

Heat up 1 tablespoon of olive oil in a large frying pan, then place the cod fillets skin-side down in the pan. Pour some water (about 100ml) over the fillets, along with the squeeze of lemon juice and the chopped garlic and parsley.

Add some salt to the water when it starts to simmer. Cook on a medium heat for about 10 minutes, gently shaking the pan now and then.

Place the olives in the pan and keep on cooking for another 5 minutes.

Lift the fillets onto a plate, pour the sauce from the pan over them and serve with the olives while still hot.

Mamma says

For extra flavour, add 15–20 halved cherry tomatoes and replace the water with a generous sprinkling of white wine (about 50–60ml).

Roasted cod skewers

Spiedini di merluzzo nero al forno

Serves: 4
Prep: 10–15 mins
Cooking: 15–20 mins

It can be a good idea to present fish to children in an imaginative way so that they're intrigued and will want to taste it; in this recipe, the cod has been speared on skewers.

I have used black cod below, but you can use normal cod, lemon sole, plaice or sea bass fillets instead.

100g breadcrumbs
50g grated Parmesan
Finely grated zest
of 1 lemon
3 sprigs of flat parsley
leaves, chopped
Olive oil
4 black cod or other
firm fish fillets
(about 100–150g
each), skinned
2 tsp capers, chopped
Sea salt
Lemon juice
Lemon wedges, to
serve (optional)

Preheat the oven to 200°C/Gas 6.

Mix the breadcrumbs, Parmesan, lemon zest, parsley and 1 tablespoon of olive oil in a bowl.

Cut the fish fillets in half lengthways and toss them in the breadcrumb mixture until they are well coated on both sides.

Spoon some chopped capers and the remaining breadcrumb mixture onto the central part of the half-fillets, then roll them and thread them onto skewers, making sure the pieces aren't quite touching. Add some salt and sprinkle with olive oil and lemon juice.

Arrange the skewers on a baking tray lined with baking parchment. Put the tray in the oven for 15–20 minutes, or until the fish is cooked through, turning the skewers over halfway through the cooking.

Serve immediately, with lemon wedges on the side, if you like.

Mamma says

To give some extra flavour, you can add chopped pitted black olives to the capers.

You can serve the fish skewers with a bed of roasted peppers, courgettes, tomatoes or aubergines. If you're planning to do that, chop the vegetables first into medium cubes (about 3cm). Place them – together with a sliced onion – in a roasting tray. Drizzle on some olive oil, then place the fish skewers on top and proceed with the cooking. It will be a fantastic main dish.

Sea bass in a salt crust

Spigola sotto sale

Serves: 4
Prep: 5 mins
Cooking: about 1 hour

My father once told me how, before refrigerators and freezers became a common presence in every household, fish was preserved in salt. As a teenager, after a week's work at sea in a fishing boat, he would bring home a few kilos of anchovies as a food reserve for the months ahead. The fish, without being washed, was gutted and placed on a layer of coarse sea salt in tall earthenware pots. A new layer of salt was added on top, then another one of fish and so on. The fish was weighed down by heavy stones for around two weeks so that it would release its moisture. It would then be ready to be dried and preserved.

In this traditional recipe, salt forms the coating in which the fish is baked. As ever, the success of the dish depends entirely on the freshness of the fish. Children love the task of packing the fish in salt, and then digging it out from the salt crust later.

1kg rock salt
1 large sea bass (about 1.2kg), gutted but with head, skin and scales left on
Olive oil
3 sprigs of flat parsley leaves, chopped
2 carrots, cut into rounds
1 lemon, sliced

Preheat the oven to 180°C/Gas 4. Place a sheet of baking parchment on a baking tray and cover it with half of the rock salt. Lay the sea bass on top and cover it with the remaining salt, making sure that none of the fish is visible. Seal the tray tightly with a sheet of foil.

Put the tray in the oven for about 1 hour. If you are not sure whether the sea bass is cooked, prod it with a cocktail stick here and there. If it's cooked, the cocktail stick will enter the flesh easily.

Remove the foil and break the salt crust open with a knife or fork. Remove all salt crystals from the surface of the fish, which at this point will be tasty and moist.

Place the sea bass on a plate and fillet it. Sprinkle over some olive oil and chopped parsley and garnish with slices of lemon and carrot before serving.

Mamma says

For the perfect side, try the potato salad with shallots from page 66.

Steam-cooked tuna steak

Tonno a bagnomaria

Serves: 4
Prep: 5 mins
Cooking: 40 mins

I love cooking fish in a bain-marie, as it brings out all its flavour, subtly blending it with the rest of the ingredients. Whoever invented this technique must have been either a mother or a genius. Or both.

When our children were very young, I prepared many bain-marie dishes, since food cooked in this way is healthy and easy for little stomachs to digest. A bain-marie is nothing more than a hot-water steam bath: you won't need any special cookware, just a normal cooking pot part-filled with boiling water and, on top of it, a plate with the food covered by a lid (or another plate).

One great advantage of this technique is that the food, not being exposed to excessive heat, better retains its texture and flavour. The only disadvantage is that it requires a longer cooking time, which is not ideal for busy mums. However, cooking thin fillets or steaks doesn't take very long, so I really recommend a bain-marie for steaming not only tuna but also any other thin pieces of fish and meat.

8 bay leaves
Olive oil
4 tuna steaks
 (1cm thick, about
 100–120g each)
100g breadcrumbs
1 tsp fresh oregano
 (or ½ tsp dried)
2 tbsp capers
Sea salt
A little lemon juice

Place the bay leaves on a large flat plate and drizzle some olive oil on top.

Wash the fish under running water and dry with kitchen paper. Place on the plate and top with the breadcrumbs, oregano and capers. Season with salt and drizzle on a little more olive oil.

Bring a half-filled pot of water to the boil. Place the plate with the tuna on top of it and cover with a lid or another plate, making sure it's airtight. Turn the heat down so the water is simmering and leave the fish to cook in the bain-marie for about 40 minutes.

Serve the fish while still hot, with a squeeze of lemon juice over it.

Mamma says

If the tuna steaks do not fit on one plate, run 2 bain-marie pots at the same time and split the seasoning equally between them.

Sweet-and-sour tuna

Tonno all'agrodolce

Serves: 4
Prep & cooking:
   10 mins

Sweet-and-sour sauces have been used for centuries in Southern Italy and Sicily, as it was a combination particularly favoured by the Arabs who once dominated the area. The sweetness was obtained by the use of honey and the sourness from citrus fruit, two readily available ingredients.

The trick for this sweet-and-sour tuna is to create a perfect blend between the two contrasting flavours. A friend of mine once told me that you have achieved the right balance when the sweet and the sour can no longer be tasted, but are imperceptibly mixed.

4 tuna steaks
   (2–3cm thick)
4 tbsp white flour
Olive oil
3 tbsp white wine
   vinegar
2 tbsp sugar
2 red onions, sliced
Sea salt

In a bowl, toss the tuna steaks in flour until they are well coated on both sides.

Heat 1 tablespoon of olive oil in a frying pan over a medium heat. Place the tuna steaks in the pan to brown for a few minutes, then lift them onto a plate lined with kitchen paper. Set the pan aside.

Mix the vinegar and the sugar in a glass.

Return the pan to to the heat, then tip in the onions and season with sea salt. Pour the contents of the glass into the pan and cook for a couple of minutes, until the onions are glossy and translucent, tossing every now and then.

Place the tuna steaks back in the pan and reduce the heat. Leave them to absorb the flavours for a couple of minutes.

Take the pan off the heat and leave the sweet-and-sour tuna to cool a little before serving.

Mamma says

If your children don't like onions, you could scatter a bit of chopped parsley over the cooked tuna instead.

Salmon with green sauce

Salmone in salsa verde

Serves: 4
Prep & cooking:
  25 mins

Salmon is a bit of a wonder-food for health, but when I first tried it out on my children, they pulled faces. I wondered if this had anything to do with the pink colour, and tried serving it with a green sauce. Initially they were suspicious – but when they tasted it they brightened up and the salmon was gone in no time.

I know I won't get a star sticker from my mamma, the purist, who believes that fish should be served only with a drizzle of olive oil and a sprinkle of salt, but this green sauce was a real revelation. Sometimes, success favours the brave in the kitchen.

4 salmon fillets (about
  150g each), skinned
½ lemon
Sea salt
1 carrot, chopped
1 celery stalk, chopped
½ onion, sliced
3 springs of flat parsley
  leaves, finely chopped
7 cherry tomatoes,
  halved
1 bay leaf
Lemon wedges, to
  serve (optional)

For the green sauce
A bunch of flat parsley
  (40g), chopped
3 tbsp capers
1½ garlic cloves
3 tbsp white wine
  vinegar
40g breadcrumbs
100ml olive oil
200g good-quality
  mayonnaise

Rub the salmon with the cut side of the lemon half, then place it in a frying pan, along with 100ml water and a pinch of salt. Add the carrot, celery, onion, parsley, tomatoes and bay leaf. Cover the pan with a lid and simmer for about 20 minutes over a medium heat, until the salmon is cooked through.

Meanwhile, to prepare the green sauce, place the chopped parsley – the whole bunch, stalks as well as leaves – in a blender with the capers, garlic, vinegar, breadcrumbs and olive oil. Blend everything until you get a smooth mixture.

Pour the mixture into a bowl and combine it with the mayonnaise to make the green sauce.

Once the salmon is ready, remove it from the pan and place it on a plate. Serve it hot with with the green sauce and some lemon wedges on the side, if you like.

Mamma says

You can create a lighter version of the sauce just by blending together some parsley, olive oil, lemon juice and a pinch of salt.

The salmon is very good with vegetables such as asparagus spears, or the roasted peppers on page 72.

Sole cooked in three ways

Sogliola in tre modi

With its mild, buttery flavour, sole is one of the best-tasting fishes around, and children adore it. For that reason I'd like to suggest three different ways of preparing it.

Ideally, use skinned sole fillets, as children can be fussy about the skin – one of the two reasons, together with bones, why kids are often reluctant to eat fish.

Sole cooked in clarified butter

Serves: 4
Prep: 5 mins
Cooking: 3–4 mins

Clarified butter is ideal for frying, as it doesn't burn at higher temperatures, and is great for people with an intolerance to lactose. You will end up with more than you need in this recipe, so save the rest for another use.

For the clarified butter
120g unsalted butter

For the sole
Milk
100g white flour
4 lemon sole fillets,
  skinned
A little lemon juice
3 sprigs of flat parsley
  leaves, chopped
Sea salt

Clarified butter is very easy to prepare. Heat up the butter in a pan at a low temperature until it melts. Skim off all the white foam from the surface with a spoon. With the aid of a filter or mesh strainer, pour the liquid butterfat into a heatproof, air-tight container and discard the milky residue. The cooled clarified butter can be stored in the fridge, covered, for up to 3 weeks (you can also freeze it).

Next, prepare the sole fillets. Put a little milk and the flour in separate bowls. Dip the fillets in the milk, then coat them with flour on both sides.

In a frying pan, heat up the clarified butter and cook the fillets for 3-4 minutes, gently turning over so they turn golden-brown on both sides.

Sprinkle some lemon juice, chopped parsley and sea salt over the fried fillets, and serve hot.

Pan-fried sole

Serves: 4
Prep: 25 mins
Cooking: 5 mins

This is the quickest and simplest way to cook your sole fillets,
as well as being a reliable hit with younger children.

4 lemon sole fillets,
  skinned
Olive oil
A little lemon juice
Sea salt
1 egg
100g white flour

Marinate the sole fillets in 3–4 tablespoons of olive oil, a squeeze
of lemon juice and a little sea salt for about 20 minutes.

Crack and whisk the egg in a bowl. Put the flour in a separate bowl.
Remove the fillets from the marinade, then roll them in the egg and
coat them with flour on both sides.

Heat up 2 tablespoons of olive oil in a frying pan and fry the fillets
for 3–4 minutes, turning gently so they turn golden-brown on both
sides. Sprinkle with sea salt and serve hot.

Sole gratin

Serves: 4
Prep: 5 mins
Cooking: 15 mins

Despite being quick and easy to do, cooking sole in a gratin is
a sophisticated way of presenting the fish – and it creates a
deliciously subtle taste.

Olive oil
4 lemon sole fillets,
  skinned
50g breadcrumbs
1 tbsp grated Parmesan
3 sprigs of flat parsley
  leaves, chopped
1 garlic clove, chopped
Sea salt

Preheat the oven to 180°C/Gas 4. Grease a baking tray with olive
oil and place the sole fillets on it.

Mix the breadcrumbs, Parmesan, parsley, garlic and a little sea
salt in a bowl.

Cover the fillets with the mixture. Drizzle over some olive oil
and then place the tray in the preheated oven for approximately
15 minutes. All done!

Swordfish rolls

Involtini di pesce spada

Serves: 4
Prep: 15 mins
Cooking: 10–15 mins

Preparing these *involtini* is not difficult, but it is essential to have the swordfish steaks cut very thin. This can be tricky to do at home, so let your fishmonger handle it for you.

The other day, when he saw me enter his shop, our fishmonger gave me his usual anxious glance. This turned into a look of terror when I asked him to cut four swordfish steaks no more than half a centimetre thick. The poor man's face became tense; he struggled to keep his hand steady while slicing the fish. But all was well in the end – and when I went home, all that I had to do was to give the steaks a little bash and cut them in half, ready to be filled and rolled.

4 vine tomatoes
1 tbsp capers
4 tbsp pitted green
  olives
1 garlic clove
12 basil leaves
2 tbsp breadcrumbs,
  plus extra for
  scattering
Fine salt
Olive oil
4 thin swordfish steaks
  (0.5cm thick, about
  150g each)
4 lemon slices
  (optional)

Preheat the oven to 160°C/Gas 3. Cut 2 of the tomatoes in half and remove the internal seeds, then chop them up and place them in a bowl. Finely chop the capers, olives, garlic and 4 of the basil leaves, and tip them into the bowl. Next add the breadcrumbs, some salt and 1 tablespoon of olive oil, and mix well.

Bash the swordfish steaks between 2 pieces of cling film or baking parchment to make them slightly thinner, then cut them in half lengthways. Spoon some of the mixture onto the central part of each piece. Roll up each steak and pin it together with a cocktail stick (or two) – it is important that each roll is properly sealed.

Slice the remaining 2 tomatoes. Skewer a slice of tomato and a basil leaf on the cocktail stick of each roll.

Line a baking tray with baking parchment. Place all the swordfish rolls on it – drizzle on a little olive oil and scatter some breadcrumbs on top. Put the tray in the preheated oven for 10–15 minutes. Serve the rolls immediately, with the slices of lemon, if you like.

Mamma says

The roasted peppers on page 72 are excellent with swordfish rolls.

Since swordfish may contain traces of mercury, this recipe is not appropriate for children under the age of five.

Swordfish in tomato sauce

Pesce spada alla salsa di pomodoro

Serves: 4
Prep: 25 mins
Cooking: 35 mins

This is a classic sweet-and-sour recipe from Sicily, which has been adopted into Puglian cuisine. Whenever I cook it, I keep some of the sauce for dressing a pasta dish the following day.

Since the swordfish steaks don't have to be cut too thin for this recipe, my fishmonger can relax – for once.

Olive oil
4 swordfish steaks
(1cm thick, about
100–120g each)
50g white flour
500g firm-textured
potatoes (such as
Charlotte), peeled
and thinly sliced

For the tomato sauce
Olive oil
1 garlic clove, chopped
½ onion, sliced
1 x 400g tin plum
tomatoes
1 celery stalk, chopped
1 tbsp capers
1 tbsp raisins
50g pitted black olives,
chopped
1 tbsp pine kernels
Chilli flakes (optional)
Sea salt
Black pepper

To prepare the tomato sauce, heat up 1 tablespoon of olive oil in a saucepan over a medium heat. Sauté the garlic and the onion, then tip the tinned tomatoes into the pan. Add the celery, capers, raisins, olives, pine kernels and chilli flakes (if using), then season. Pour in 150ml water, cover, and bring to the boil. Simmer for about 20 minutes, uncovered, until the sauce thickens. If you like, add a little more salt, to taste, while cooking.

Meanwhile, heat up 2 tablespoons of olive oil in a frying pan over a medium heat. Toss the swordfish steaks in the flour until they are well coated on both sides. Remove any excess flour and place them in the frying pan to brown on each side – this will take just a few minutes.

Lift the swordfish steaks onto a plate and add the thinly sliced potatoes to the frying pan, together with 1 tablespoon more of olive oil. Cook them for about 15 minutes over a low heat, stirring occasionally, until the potatoes have softened and mostly cooked through. Meanwhile, preheat the oven to 180°C/Gas 4.

Remove the potatoes from the pan and use them to cover the base of a baking tray greased with olive oil. Lay the swordfish steaks on the potatoes and cover the steaks with the tomato sauce. Put the tray in the preheated oven for 15 minutes. Serve hot.

Mamma says

Like any other fish, swordfish should be eaten within 24 hours of purchasing. Avoid serving swordfish to children under five years of age, as it may contain traces of mercury.

Pan-cooked prawns with tomatoes

Gamberetti al pomodoro

Serves: 4
Prep & cooking:
20 mins

When my mamma goes to the local fish market in Italy, the children often accompany her. Once they get there, they dart around from one stall to another like little imps, wanting to know the names of each and every fish, and to spot one that is still twitching. They are particularly fascinated by lobsters and prawns – which are also among their favourite kinds of seafood.

This recipe is light, healthy and quick. There's no frying: you just add all your ingredients to the pan, mix them together, let them stew briefly, and the dish is ready to enjoy. Simply delicious.

Olive oil
½ onion, sliced
2 garlic cloves,
  chopped
800g raw shell-on king
  prawns, washed
20 cherry tomatoes,
  chopped
1 celery stalk, chopped
3 sprigs of flat parsley
  leaves, chopped
Sea salt
100ml white wine

Pour 2 tablespoons of olive oil into a frying pan, along with the onion, garlic, prawns, tomatoes, celery and parsley, then season with sea salt. Pour in the white wine and mix all the ingredients with the help of two spoons. Cook on a medium heat with the lid on for about 10 minutes, stirring from time to time.

Serve the prawns with a generous dressing of sauce from the pan and plenty of fresh bread, as I am sure you and your children will want to mop up all the sauce!

Mamma says

For the best results, buy the prawns on the same day as you are planning to cook them.

For younger children or if your kids are fussy about the idea of unshelled prawns, I suggest you shell and chop the prawns before serving. You can also use peeled prawns instead, either raw or cooked (the cooking time will be the same for both).

Fried seafood

Frittura

Serves: 4
Prep: 15 mins
Cooking: 15 mins

Few people know that fried seafood is one of the most popular dishes in Italy. At the weekend, the discerning fish eaters of Puglia will go to their favourite restaurant by the sea and order a *frittura di paranza* (the name derives from a particular kind of fishing boat) made with small fish such as codlings, baby mullets, baby soles and anchovies.

My recipe does not involve any *paranza* fish, but only peeled uncooked prawns and squid rings – a safe choice, since children tend to love them.

300g squid rings
200g raw peeled
 king prawns
Sunflower oil, for
 deep-frying
100–150g '00' white
 flour
Fine salt
Juice of 1 lemon
 (optional)

Make sure the squid rings and prawns are dry by patting them with kitchen paper.

Pour plenty of sunflower oil into a deep pan so it is no more than a third full, and heat to a frying temperature of 180°C (or when a cube of bread turns golden-brown in a minute; if it browns too quickly, turn down the heat slightly).

Meanwhile, dip 5–6 squid rings or prawns at a time in the flour, coating both sides of the seafood. Carefully lower into the hot oil and fry until slightly golden. Remove from the pan and leave to drain on a plate lined with kitchen paper. Repeat the procedure until you have used all your squid rings and prawns.

Sprinkle over some fine salt and serve hot. If you wish, squeeze a few drops of lemon juice on the *frittura*.

Mamma says

Our friend Antonio once gave me a tip which I am only too glad to pass on to you. For extra lightness, he suggested dipping the squid rings and prawns in a mixture of egg white and sparkling water (2 egg whites and 100ml sparkling water) before coating them with flour and frying them.

Lobster tails in tomato sauce

Code di aragosta al sugo

Serves: 4
Prep & cooking:
  30 mins

Code di aragosta is one of the most sophisticated – verging on decadent – offerings of our cuisine. It is equally good for dinner parties or a family gathering: we often have it on Christmas Eve ahead of a big meal the following day, and it never fails to get us in the festive spirit.

Sometimes it's hard to decide what kind of lobster to buy and how to cook it. This simple recipe will solve both problems and avoid a repeat of the *Annie Hall* lobster scene in your kitchen.

Lobster has such a delicate flavour that it will need very little seasoning. As with other fish and seafood, less is more.

Olive oil
1 garlic clove, chopped
1 shallot, finely sliced
4 lobster tails,
  shells removed
100ml white wine
200g tinned plum
  tomatoes
500ml passata
Sea salt
3 sprigs of flat parsley
  leaves, chopped
Black pepper
Bread or toast, to serve

Heat up 1 tablespoon of olive oil in a large saucepan and in it sauté the garlic and shallot, stirring occasionally, until translucent.

Cut the lobster tails into 4–5cm pieces and add them to the saucepan. Let them brown for 2–3 minutes, stirring from time to time.

Add the white wine to the saucepan and, continuing to stir, simmer on low heat until most of the liquid has evaporated. Next, pour in the tinned tomatoes and passata. Add a glass of water (about 150ml), a pinch of salt, half of the chopped parsley and some freshly ground black pepper. Bring to the boil, then cook for about 20 minutes on a low heat, stirring occasionally, until the sauce is smooth and thick.

Once cooked, cover the lobster tails with a generous helping of sauce and scatter the rest of the parsley on top. Serve with fresh or toasted bread. (Any leftover sauce can be eaten with pasta later.)

Mamma says

Instead of serving this with bread, you can try it as a wonderfully rich sauce for linguine, spaghetti or paccheri pasta, as in the photograph opposite.

The parsley can be replaced with 3 chopped basil leaves. If you can't find lobster tails at a fishmonger's, use 500g king prawns and 300g langoustines (shell them before serving).

Stuffed squid with potatoes

Calamari ripieni al forno con patate

Serves: 4
Prep: 15 mins
Cooking: 35 mins

The first time I prepared this dish for Alessandro, when we were only just married, I saw him turn the squid over and over with his fork. 'Is anything the matter?' I said. 'I thought you liked squid.'

'Oh, I adore it.'

'Then what?'

'I was just curious,' he said. 'You see, in the region where I come from, we don't stuff... the stuff... We only grill it or fry it.' That was when I realised how distinctively Puglian this recipe is.

Although you can prepare the squid yourself at home, I suggest you ask your fishmonger to do it, in order to avoid the mess.

Do not use New Zealand squid or frozen ones, as the dish will lose all of its flavour.

Olive oil

500g firm-textured
potatoes (such as
Charlotte)

4 prepared medium
squid (with or without
tentacles)

1 tbsp grated Pecorino
Romano

1 garlic clove, finely
chopped

3 sprigs of flat parsley
leaves, chopped

75g breadcrumbs

1 egg, whisked

Sea salt

Preheat the oven to 180°C/Gas 4. Grease a baking dish with olive oil.

Peel the potatoes and cut them into slices about 2mm thick. Lay out the slices on the greased tray.

Rinse the squid under cold water and dry them with kitchen paper. If your squid have tentacles, cut them off. Chop the tentacles from 2 of the squid into small pieces, leaving the other tentacles whole.

Put the Pecorino, garlic, parsley and two thirds (around 50g) of the breadcrumbs into a bowl and add the chopped tentacles, if using. Add the whisked egg and mix well.

With a teaspoon, fill the sac of each squid until it is about two-thirds full, then close with a cocktail stick – or 2 cocktail sticks, threaded through the top in a diagonal cross. Do not overfill the squids.

Place the stuffed squid on top of the potatoes (along with the whole tentacles, if using). Finish with some olive oil, a pinch of salt and the rest of the breadcrumbs, then bake for 35 minutes.

Use a fork to check if the squid is tender, then serve it hot with the cocktail sticks removed.

Octopus salad

Insalata di polpo

Serves: 4
Prep: 15 mins
Cooking: 45 mins
  (or longer, depending
  on the octopus)

This is one of the highlights of Puglian cuisine, a perfect summer dish that can be served as either a starter or a main course.

Finding fresh octopus in the UK can be a challenge, but it's something that children are likely to adore because of its delicate flavour. If your local fishmonger doesn't stock Mediterranean octopus (often sold in frozen packs), you can buy the small, Atlantic variety instead, which is quite tender compared to the ones found in Puglian markets; the good news is that you won't have to bash it against the rocks or cook it for over an hour to get it soft and moist. Either way, ask your fishmonger to prepare the octopus for you.

A 600–750g prepared
Mediterranean (or
  Atlantic) octopus
Sea salt
1 tbsp white wine
  vinegar
400g firm-textured
  potatoes (such as
  Charlotte), peeled
  and roughly chopped
Olive oil
1 celery stalk, roughly
  chopped
½–1 tbsp chopped
  basil, to taste
Black pepper

Rinse the octopus under cold water and place it in a large cooking pot filled with water. Add 1 teaspoon of sea salt and the vinegar, then bring the water to the boil and let it simmer for about 1 hour 10 minutes, or until tender – cook for half an hour less (40 minutes) if the octopus has been frozen or if it is an Atlantic octopus.

Meanwhile, place the potatoes in a large, deep frying pan (about 30cm in diameter) with 1½ tablespoons of olive oil and the chopped celery stalk. Add enough water to cover, put a lid on the pan and leave to cook for about 20–25 minutes on a low heat, until the potatoes are tender. Drain off any excess liquid.

When the octopus is ready, remove it from the pot and cool it down under running water. Cut the tentacles into pieces, slice the head into 2cm rings and mix the octopus with the potatoes in the frying pan. Cook for 5 minutes over a medium-low heat, so all the flavours can blend together. Before serving, add 1 tablespoon of olive oil, a pinch of salt, the chopped basil and some black pepper.

Leave the salad to rest, then serve at room temperature.

Mamma says

For great salad variations, try adding chopped parsley, sliced fennel, black olives or halved cherry tomatoes at the end.

Oven-baked octopus with potatoes

Polpo con patate al forno

Serves: 4
Prep: 15–20 mins
Cooking: 45 mins
(or longer, depending on the octopus)

If I had to pick just one dish that reminds me of my mamma's cooking, it would be *polpo con patate al forno*, a typical Puglian recipe usually cooked in an earthenware pot. All I can say is that this is my Proustian 'madeleine moment' – and I hope you can also enjoy this dish many times with your family and friends.

Ask your fishmonger to prepare the octopus for you. If you can't find fresh Mediterranean octopus, you can use the smaller Atlantic variety, which is equally delicious and slightly more tender. During the cooking process, the octopus will release some water, so don't worry if you see some liquid at the bottom of the tray; this will give the potatoes a lovely flavour. There is even a saying in the Molfettese dialect: 'Every octopus will cook in its own water,' which applies to stubborn people who should be left to stew in their own juice.

A 600–750g prepared Mediterranean (or Atlantic) octopus
Olive oil
1 shallot, chopped
3 sprigs of flat parsley leaves, finely chopped
100ml white wine
10 cherry tomatoes, halved
400g red or firm-textured potatoes (such as Desiree or Charlotte)
Sea salt
Pecorino Romano
2 tbsp breadcrumbs

Preheat the oven to 200°C/Gas 6. Rinse the octopus under cold water, cut the tentacles into pieces and slice the head into rings.

Grease the base of a ceramic baking dish with olive oil. Scatter on the shallot and half of the parsley. Lay the octopus pieces in the dish, then add the white wine and cherry tomatoes.

Now peel the potatoes and cut them into slices about 2mm thick. Use them to cover the octopus pieces completely, then season with sea salt.

Drizzle on a little olive oil, then grate on some Pecorino, and scatter over the breadcrumbs and the rest of the chopped parsley. Put the tray in the preheated oven for about 45 minutes, or until the octopus is tender.

Serve hot, with a slice of toast for each person.

Mamma says

Take care not to add too much salt to the potatoes, otherwise it will overwhelm the natural flavour of the octopus.

Calamari rings with tomato sauce

Calamarata

Serves: 4
Prep & cooking:
40 mins

This light and tasty dish – a long-time favourite of our children's – can be served on its own or with fresh or toasted bread. It can also be used as a dressing for paccheri pasta, whose texture and oversized tubular shape are ideal for absorbing the fish sauce.

If there are no fresh calamari rings on offer at the fish counter, don't despair: you can always ask your patient fishmonger to clean a whole squid and slice its body into 2–3cm rings for you. I often do that, with a ladylike smile, and he never complains.

Olive oil
2 garlic cloves,
  chopped
500g calamari rings
3 sprigs of flat parsley
  leaves, finely chopped
Sea salt
50ml white wine
1 x 400g tin plum
  tomatoes

Heat up 1 tablespoon of olive oil in a saucepan and in it sauté the chopped garlic cloves. Add the calamari rings, the parsley and a pinch of sea salt to the saucepan, then pour in the white wine. Leave to simmer for about 10 minutes, stirring now and then, until most of the liquid has evaporated.

Next, tip in the tinned tomatoes and a small glass of water (about 100ml). Use the back of a wooden spoon to crush and squeeze the tomatoes so they make a rough sauce. Cook for another 25 minutes, until the sauce becomes smooth and thick.

Serve the calamari and sauce while still hot.

Mamma says

For this recipe I prefer to use a tin of peeled plum tomatoes rather than passata, because the thinner liquid works better in the cooking process and the slight acidity of the tomatoes makes them a better match with fish and seafood.

If you and your children don't mind spicy food, you can add some chilli flakes for extra flavour. For my husband, this is a must.

Baby cuttlefish with peas

Seppioline con piselli

Serves: 4
Prep: 10 mins
Cooking: 1 hour

This is perfect as a light, healthy dinner. Preparation is quick, but the cooking time is pretty long, so either read a book or run yourself a hot scented bath while it cooks. Alternatively use a pressure cooker, like most of my friends do.

A pressure cooker will cut down the time and energy needed to cook your food by about half. Some claim that, due to the shorter cooking time, the nutritional value of the ingredients is better preserved and the food retains more of its moisture. If you do decide to use a pressure cooker, read the manufacturer's instructions carefully before starting out.

×××××××××××××××××××××××××××××××××

500g prepared baby cuttlefish (or baby squid)
Olive oil
½ onion, finely chopped
1 carrot, finely chopped
1 celery stalk, finely sliced
1 garlic clove, finely chopped
3 sprigs of flat parsley leaves, chopped
1 bay leaf
Chilli flakes (optional)
100ml white wine
200g frozen peas
200g cherry tomatoes, halved
Sea salt

Rinse the baby cuttlefish (or squid) under cold water, slice their bodies into rings and leave them in a colander to dry.

Heat up 1 tablespoon of olive oil in a large saucepan over a medium heat. Add the onion and leave it to sizzle until it's translucent. Add the carrot, celery, garlic, parsley, bay leaf and the chilli flakes, if using.

Place the cuttlefish in the saucepan and sprinkle in the white wine. Let the dish simmer for about 15 minutes, until most of the liquid has evaporated, then add the peas, cherry tomatoes and 200ml water, and season with sea salt.

Stir all the ingredients and cover the saucepan with a lid. Bring to the boil, then turn down the heat and simmer, uncovered, for another 45 minutes. Serve while still hot.

Mamma says

For extra flavour, add the zest of a lemon and 2 tablespoons of passata with the peas and the cherry tomatoes.

Meat

In the old days, a family's menu for the main meal of the day was usually arranged according to a regular pattern: fish or vegetable soups on Mondays and Saturdays, pasta on Tuesdays, Thursdays and Sundays, legumes on Wednesdays, vegetables on Fridays and meat – perhaps by necessity – only on Sundays.

This tradition has partially continued to our day, and meat, which is an essential ingredient in other parts of Italy, doesn't play such a central role in Puglian cuisine. Our mammas' culinary creativity has focused on pasta, fish and vegetable dishes, and these tend to dominate as main courses.

I have always had a complicated relationship with meat. The memory of the horse steaks administered by my mother for the purpose of improving my blood iron levels still brings me out in a cold sweat from time to time. Lamb, on the other hand, has the opposite effect on me, associated as it is with family gatherings and joyful celebration: Easter wouldn't be Easter in Puglia without lamb, the indispensable ingredient for an Easter Sunday ragù. From the early hours of each festive day, the ragù sauce's distinctive smell fills the streets of Molfetta's old *borgo*.

There are many excellent meat dishes in our cuisine, and I'd like to share some of them with you. As well as creating some variety in the kitchen, they are easy to make and will help provide a balanced diet for the whole family.

Juicy chicken with peas

Pollo e piselli

Serves: 4
Prep: 5 mins
Cooking: 20 mins

Among the ingredients that should always be available in a busy mum's kitchen are chicken, milk and frozen peas. Children, babies and toddlers adore *pollo e piselli*, and even the pickiest husband will eat it ungrudgingly.

4 skinned chicken
  breast fillets (300g)
2 tbsp white flour
Olive oil
¼ onion, finely sliced
250g frozen peas
½ vegetable stock cube
Sea salt
150ml milk

Cut the chicken breasts into escalopes about 1cm thick and toss them in flour, shaking off any excess.

Heat some olive oil in a saucepan and sauté the onion until it becomes translucent. Stir in the frozen peas with a wooden spoon.

Now add a glass of water (about 150ml), the half vegetable stock cube and a pinch of sea salt. Cover with a lid and leave to cook for about 7–8 minutes, checking now and then that the water has not totally evaporated, otherwise the peas will get burnt.

Meanwhile, heat up 2 more tablespoons of olive oil in a frying pan and add the chicken fillets coated in flour. Cook them on both sides until they start to turn golden. Check that the chicken is cooked, then sprinkle on some salt and pour in the milk. Let it simmer for a few minutes, until the milk has almost totally evaporated.

At this point add the onion and peas to the chicken in the pan and leave to cook for another 2–3 minutes, so that all the flavours can blend together. Serve hot.

Mamma says

This is a versatile recipe, and you can replace the peas with any other vegetable you dig out from the fridge, such as asparagus, courgettes or carrots. It also works well with turkey, which remains moist and juicy thanks to the milk.

Chicken burgers

Hamburger di pollo e patate

Serves: 4
Prep: 25–30 mins
Cooking: 10–12 mins
  (or 20 mins if baking)

All children love burgers, and it's great if you can give them homemade ones. I must once again thank my ever-resourceful sister-in-law, Isabella, for this brilliant recipe.

  If you don't have a meat mincer in your kitchen, I suggest you buy minced chicken from your butcher (or local supermarket if they have it in stock). You may be better off phoning ahead to place your order, as the butcher may need to clean the grinder in order to mince a different kind of meat – and that takes time.

3 floury or all-purpose
  potatoes (such as
  King Edward or Maris
  Piper)
400g chicken mince
1 egg
30g grated Parmesan
30g breadcrumbs
Fine salt
Olive oil (if frying)

To serve
4 burger buns
2 beef tomatoes, sliced
Lettuce leaves
Ketchup (optional)

Boil the unpeeled potatoes until tender. Drain in a colander and leave to cool.

Peel the potatoes and mash them in a bowl, then add the chicken mince, egg, Parmesan and breadcrumbs. Season with salt and mix everything together well.

Split the mixture into 4 equal-sized balls, then press each ball down and mould it into a burger shape. Now you can choose your cooking method – the result is equally tasty, but frying the burgers is quicker and baking them is healthier.

To fry the burgers: Heat some olive oil in a frying pan, then add the burgers and cover. Cook the burgers for 10–12 minutes, turning them halfway, until they are golden-brown and cooked through to the centre.

To bake the burgers: Preheat the oven to 200°C/Gas 6. Place the burgers on a baking tray greased with olive oil. Put the tray in the oven for about 20 minutes, until the burgers are cooked through.

In both cases, serve hot in the burger buns with slices of tomato and some lettuce. For extra flavour, add a little ketchup.

Mamma says

For lighter burgers, use only the white of the egg.

Breaded chicken escalopes
Cotolette

Serves: 4
Prep: 5 mins
Cooking: 10 mins

The recipe for *cotolette* is ancient, possibly dating back to the Middle Ages, and it has remained one of the most popular dishes across all the Italian regions. It has also found its way to our kitchen table in both Puglia and London.

The original Milanese *cotoletta* with veal – probably named after the French *côtelette*, or 'cutlet' – is bashed for a few minutes, rolled in beaten eggs and breadcrumbs, fried in clarified butter and served with foil wrapped around the bone.

In my mamma's version, breaded chicken escalopes are fried in olive oil rather than butter. I have always followed her recipe with great success.

4 skinned chicken
 breast fillets
50g white flour
2 eggs
1 tbsp grated Parmesan
Fine salt
100g breadcrumbs
Olive oil
Lemon slices, to serve

Cut the chicken breasts into escalopes about 1cm thick and bash them between sheets of baking parchment or cling film to make them flat and tender. Next, toss them in flour until they are well coated on both sides. Shake off any excess flour.

Crack the eggs into a bowl and whisk them. Add the Parmesan and mix with the eggs. Season with fine salt.

Spread the breadcrumbs on a flat plate. Roll the escalopes in the beaten eggs, then coat them with breadcrumbs on both sides.

Heat 2 tablespoons of olive oil in a frying pan over a medium heat. Fry the escalopes on both sides until they turn golden-brown and are cooked through.

Serve the *cotolette* hot, with slices of lemon.

Mamma says

You can serve this dish with fries or a green salad. Our children like to eat a *cotoletta* in a bread roll with tomato, cucumber and lettuce, as if it were a chicken burger.

For extra flavour, add a teaspoon of ground nutmeg to the egg mixture. If you get tired tired of chicken, use turkey instead.

Sausage-scented potatoes

Profumo di salsiccia con patate

Serves: 4
Prep & cooking:
  30 mins

We have many different types of sausage in Puglia. One especially renowned sausage is the *zampina*, a product of a town called Sammichele di Bari. Long, thin and curled, it is made of assorted meats and seasoned with Pecorino Romano cheese, parsley, chilli and tomato. I once went to the late-summer Zampina Festival in Sammichele, where I joined a meandering queue of visitors who were waiting to try the famous speciality, grilled over flaming embers. Aaah!

This recipe for potatoes with sausage meat was suggested to me by a friend, who uses veal sausages in her version. I have replaced the veal sausages with pork ones, which are easier to find in butchers' shops and supermarkets.

700g firm-textured potatoes (such as Desiree or Charlotte), peeled and chopped
Sea salt
300g pork sausages
20g unsalted butter
3 sage leaves, finely chopped
6 cherry tomatoes, halved
150ml white wine

Boil the chopped potatoes in salted water for 10 minutes. Drain and set aside on a plate.

Gently ease the skin off the sausages with the tip of a pair of scissors. Put the sausage meat in a bowl and set aside. (Discard the skins.)

Melt the butter in a frying pan over a low heat and add the sage and tomatoes. Place the meat in the pan, add a pinch of salt and stir. Now pour on the white wine and cook for about 2–3 minutes.

Next, add the potatoes to the pan and stir, then cook for another 10 minutes. Serve hot.

Mamma says

I recommend that you use plain or lightly seasoned sausages, as children usually don't like strong flavours. Don't worry about using wine in a dish for children, since most of the alcohol boils away during cooking.

Escalopes with mushrooms

Scaloppine ai funghi

Serves: 4
Prep & cooking:
15–20 mins

It's an interesting fact that often children are not too keen on mushrooms on their own, but are happy to eat them with pasta or meat. Ideally this dish should be prepared with fresh porcini mushrooms, but since they can be hard to come by, you can use chestnut or cup mushrooms and still get a fantastic result.

4 beef or veal
  escalopes (about
  400g)
2 tbsp white flour, plus
  extra for coating
Olive oil
30g unsalted butter
1 garlic clove, chopped
500g chestnut or
  cup mushrooms,
  trimmed and sliced
Sea salt
3 sprigs of flat parsley
  leaves, finely chopped

Bash the escalopes between 2 sheets of baking parchment or cling film to a thickness of about 3–4mm. Next, toss them in flour until they are well coated on both sides. Shake off any excess flour.

Heat up 2 tablespoons of olive oil in a frying pan over a medium heat. Brown the escalopes on both sides for about 5 minutes, then take off the heat and leave them in the pan, covered by a lid.

In a separate frying pan, melt the butter over a medium-high heat and sauté the garlic until it starts to brown, then add the mushrooms. When they start releasing their water, add a pinch of sea salt and the parsley. Leave everything to cook for about 10 minutes, stirring from time to time.

Now half-fill a glass with water (about 75ml) and add the 2 tablespoons of flour. Mix well before pouring the mixture into the mushroom pan. Keep on stirring until you get a creamy sauce, then add the escalopes and gently mix them with the mushrooms so that all the flavours can blend together. Serve hot.

Mamma says

As an alternative to beef or veal escalopes, you can use turkey or chicken escalopes, again bashed out to around 3–4mm thick.

Pan-fried escalopes with cherry tomatoes

Fettina di vitello alla pizzaiola

Serves: 4
Prep: 5 mins
Cooking: 10 mins

This very simple meat and tomato recipe, probably of Neapolitan origins, is perhaps the most popular meat dish in our household.

The *pizzaiola* sauce is just as tasty as the escalope itself, and the children, after eating the meat, love to mop it up with one or two pieces of bread.

Although I tend to use veal, this recipe works equally well with beef.

4 veal (or beef) escalopes, (about 400g)
Olive oil
15 cherry tomatoes, halved
1 garlic clove, chopped
3 sprigs of flat parsley leaves, chopped
2 basil leaves, shredded
Fine salt

Bash the escalopes between 2 sheets of baking parchment or cling film to a thickness of 1–2mm.

Drizzle a little olive oil into a non-stick frying pan over a medium heat. Lay the veal escalopes in the pan. Add the tomatoes, garlic, parsley and basil. Season with salt, cover with a lid and cook for about 5 minutes.

Now turn the escalopes over, sprinkle over some more salt and squash the tomatoes with the back of a wooden spoon to create a juicy sauce. Continue to cook for 4–5 minutes more.

Serve the meat covered with tomato sauce from the pan.

Mamma says

For extra flavour, you could add a sliced shallot and some chopped pitted black olives at the same time as the other sauce ingredients.

Beef and potato stew

Spezzatino con patate

Serves: 4
Prep: 15 mins
Cooking: 1 hour 10 mins

There's nothing better than a reviving bowl of stew at the end of a long winter's day. It's like a ray of sunshine through the cracks of a dark and cloudy British evening.

Any leftover stew can be stored in the fridge and warmed up the following day – it will have become even more delicious by then.

Olive oil
1 onion, sliced
1 carrot, chopped
1 celery stalk, chopped
500g beef chuck
  or beef shin, cut
  into 3–4cm pieces
3 tbsp white wine
  (or 1½ tbsp white
  wine vinegar)
100ml passata
1kg potatoes (any
  type), peeled and
  chopped
2 bay leaves
Sea salt

Heat up a little olive oil in a large saucepan over a medium-high heat. Sauté the onion until it becomes translucent.

Add the carrot and celery and then the beef to the pan. Sprinkle the white wine (or white wine vinegar) on top and leave it to brown for 5 minutes.

Now pour in the passata and around 1 litre of water. Add the potatoes and bay leaves, and season with salt.

Part-cover the saucepan with a lid and simmer on a medium-low heat for around 1 hour 10 minutes, stirring from time to time, until most of the liquid has evaporated. Make sure the heat is not too high, or the sauce will evaporate too quickly.

Serve the beef and potato stew hot.

Mamma says

If you are using a pressure cooker, cooking time will be reduced to 30-35 minutes.

If possible, always buy your meat from the local butcher, who can recommend the tastiest cuts of stewing meat available that day. If you use a different cut of meat, remember to adjust the cooking time accordingly.

Flattened meatballs with mozzarella

Schiacciatine

Serves: 4
Prep: 10 mins
Cooking: 20 mins

Schiacciatine are a typical dish from the Salento area. Their name derives from the verb *schiacciare* or 'press down', and they are nothing more and nothing less than flattened meatballs. If not a direct ancestor of the burger, the *schiacciatina* can at least be regarded as one of its distant cousins. Our children, who can be fussy meat eaters at times, are big fans of this dish, and their favourite *schiacciatine* are these mozzarella-and-ham ones.

50g soft white
  breadcrumbs
4 tbsp milk
1 egg
3 sprigs of flat parsley
  leaves, finely chopped
300g lean beef mince
2 tbsp grated Parmesan
1 tsp grated nutmeg
Fine salt
Black pepper
1 x mozzarella (125g),
  diced
50g sliced Italian
  cooked ham,
  shredded
6–12 bay leaves

Preheat the oven to 180°C/Gas 4.

In a shallow bowl, mix the breadcrumbs with the milk. Crack and whisk the egg in a separate bowl, then add the breadcrumb mixture, parsley, mince, Parmesan and nutmeg. Season with salt and pepper. Use your hands to combine all the ingredients well.

Put the mozzarella and the ham in a separate, shallow bowl.

Take a small handful of meat mixture and place some mozzarella cubes and ham shreds in the middle of it. With the other hand, take a smaller handful of meat mixture and press it on top to seal and flatten the patty. Repeat the procedure until all the meat mixture has been used. You should have about 6 medium-sized patties (or 12 small ones).

Line a ceramic baking dish with baking parchment, then lay the *schiacciatine* inside and place a bay leaf on top of each of them. Put the tray in the oven for 20 minutes.

Serve the *schiacciatine* hot.

Mamma says

Instead of breadcrumbs, you could use the soft parts of 2 thick slices of white bread: soak the bread in milk and drain it before adding to the rest of the ingredients. You can also replace the mozzarella with another cheese of your choice.

Italian meatloaf

Polpettone

Serves: 4
Prep: 15 mins
Cooking: 30–40 mins

Every Thursday night, my mamma and her friends play a game of cards: *buraco*. The interesting thing about these games is not the end result, but the improbable exchanges arising around the table between one hand and the next – as well as the making and unmaking of culinary reputations.

My *polpettone* has a simple filling of spinach – much lighter than some other versions that have been proposed at the card table… It's the perfect evening meal for rumbling stomachs.

200g fresh spinach, washed and stalks removed
A knob of unsalted butter
400g lean beef mince
30g Parmesan
3 sprigs of flat parsley leaves, finely chopped
3–5 tbsp milk
Fine salt
30g breadcrumbs
½ onion, sliced
3 cherry tomatoes, halved
Olive oil
500g firm or all-purpose potatoes (such as Charlotte or Maris Piper)
2 tsp dried oregano

Preheat the oven to 200°C/Gas 6.

Boil the spinach leaves for a few minutes in a little water. Drain, squeezing out all the water thoroughly.

Melt the butter in a frying pan over a medium heat and add the spinach leaves. Sauté them for a couple of minutes until wilted, stirring all the time. Remove the pan from the heat.

Put the mince, Parmesan, parsley and 3 tablespoons of milk in a bowl and season with salt. Use your hands to combine all the ingredients well. If they don't come together, add a bit more milk.

Transfer the meat mixture to some baking parchment. Flatten it to a rectangle about 10-12mm thick. Spread the spinach evenly over it and, using the paper, roll the meat mixture over its longer side into a loaf. Model the meatloaf further into an oblong shape and place it on a roasting tray, with the baking parchment lining the base. Scatter the breadcrumbs over, then spread the onion and the tomatoes out on top and drizzle over some olive oil.

Now peel and cut the potatoes into slices about 2-3mm thick, and arrange them around the meatloaf. Drizzle over some olive oil and scatter on the oregano.

Put the tray in the oven for 30-40 minutes, or until the meatloaf is brown and cooked through, and the potatoes tender. Serve warm.

Courgette boats

Barchette di zucchine

Serves: 4
Prep: 15 mins
Cooking: 30 mins

I am not sure that 'courgette boats' is strictly the correct name for this dish, but with a healthy imagination the courgettes could be boats waiting to sail for faraway seas – especially if you use cocktail sticks to create *tricolore* (or pirate) flags for flying above deck. Quick and easy to make, this is a perfect recipe for youthful cooks.

+ + + + + + + + + + + + + + + + +

4 courgettes
Olive oil
½ onion, sliced
Fine salt
1 egg
250g lean lamb mince
2 tbsp grated Parmesan
2 tbsp milk, plus extra
  if needed
2 tbsp breadcrumbs,
  plus extra if needed
3 sprigs of flat parsley
  leaves, finely chopped
8 cherry tomatoes,
  halved

Preheat the oven to 200°C/Gas 6.

Trim the courgettes, then cut them in half lengthways. Scoop out the pulp carefully with a spoon or melon baller; the sides and base of the 'boats' should be 1.5–2cm thick. Dice the pulp and place it in a bowl.

Heat up 2 tablespoons of olive oil in a frying pan over a medium-high heat. Sauté the onion until it is translucent, then add the courgette pulp and stir-fry for 4 minutes.

Boil the courgette boats in salted water for a minute or so to soften them, then drain and cool in a colander under cold running water. Put on a plate and pat dry with kitchen paper.

Crack and whisk the egg in a bowl. Add the mince, Parmesan, milk, breadcrumbs, parsley and courgette pulp. Season with salt and mix; the texture should be pliable but not too sticky (just add another tablespoon of milk or breadcrumbs, as needed).

Grease a ceramic baking dish with olive oil and lay the courgettes in it, hollow side up. Using a spoon, fill them with meat mixture.

On top of each courgette boat add 2 halved tomatoes and a trickle of olive oil. Bake the boats in the oven for about 30 minutes, until brown on top and cooked through. Leave to cool before serving.

Mamma says

You can try using round squashes instead – but then you'll have to come up with a new name as they won't look like boats any more...

Lamb chops braised in milk

Agnello al latte

Serves: 4
Prep: 5 mins
Cooking: 55 mins

This dish, usually prepared for important festivities such as Easter or Christmas, comes from my grandmother's recipe book. The lamb is left to cook and tenderise for about 50 minutes in milk and is then served with the resulting creamy sauce. The additional flavour of fennel seeds gives it a wonderfully delicate taste that goes well with a side dish of potato purée or salad.

For this recipe, use lamb chump chops (a cut taken from the top of the leg) with skin and excess fat removed. Alternatively, you could go for meat from the shoulder or the neck, which is ideal for slow cooking.

Olive oil
1 shallot, sliced
4 lamb chump chops
2 tbsp fennel seeds
Sea salt
250ml milk
3 sprigs of flat parsley
  leaves, finely chopped

Heat up some olive oil in a large saucepan over a medium-high heat and sauté the shallot until it becomes translucent.

Lay the lamb chops in the saucepan, and brown them slightly on both sides. Add the fennel seeds and season lightly with sea salt – more salt can be added later if necessary.

Pour the milk into the saucepan and reduce the heat. Add the chopped parsley and cover partially with a lid. Leave to simmer for 40–50 minutes, until the meat is tender. (Keep an eye on the chops and check after 35–40 minutes if they're well cooked by piercing with a fork; depending on their thickness, the chops might need less than 50 minutes.)

Serve the chops hot with a little sauce on top.

Lamb steaks with scrambled peas

Agnello con piselli

Serves: 4
Prep: 5 mins
Cooking: 1 hour

The other day Emiliano wandered into the kitchen while I was busy preparing this dish. *'Ce mangimm?'* he asked in Molfettese. I told him we were going to eat *u benedite* ('the blessed one'). He frowned, giving me a puzzled look, so I explained that this was the name traditionally given to the lamb cooked on Easter Sunday. In the olden days, the lamb would be placed in the middle of the table and the head of the family, usually the father, would bless it with an olive branch dipped in holy water provided by the local church.

The original recipe also includes pancetta cubes, but I prefer this lighter version, as the dish is quite rich already. For the same reason, I would suggest you remove any fat from the lamb steaks before cooking them.

Olive oil
1 onion, sliced
4 lamb leg steaks
Sea salt
500g frozen peas
2 eggs
3 sprigs of flat parsley
  leaves, finely chopped
50g Pecorino Romano

Heat up 2 tablespoons of olive oil in a large saucepan over a medium heat. Add the onion and leave it to sizzle until it is translucent.

Place the lamb steaks in the saucepan and sprinkle some sea salt on them. Brown the lamb on both sides.

Now add 250ml water. Cover with a lid and bring to the boil, then take the lid off and reduce the heat. Let simmer for 30–35 minutes, until most of the liquid has evaporated.

At that point, add the frozen peas and simmer with the lid on for 20 minutes more, stirring from time to time, then take off the heat.

Now crack and whisk the eggs in a bowl. Add the chopped parsley and the Pecorino and mix well.

Pour the egg mixture into the saucepan and mix briskly with the lamb and peas to obtain a scrambled texture. Serve while still hot.

Oven-baked lamb cutlets with potatoes

Agnello al forno con patate

Serves: 4
Prep: 10 mins
Cooking: 40 mins

Every time I am planning to cook lamb, I go to my trusted local butcher's, where I have been buying meat for the last ten years. Not only will he recommend the best chops and cutlets available on the day, but he will also explain the origin of every cut of meat and what you can do with the various parts of each animal.

This is a very easy dish to prepare. I tend to use cutlets – around 2cm thick, so they don't dry out – but loin chops or leg steaks will work just as well. The exact cooking time depends on the size and thickness of the pieces of lamb. The important thing is that the meat is tender and that you cook it to perfection.

Olive oil

400g cherry tomatoes, halved

8 lamb cutlets (about 700g)

Sea salt

750g firm-textured potatoes (such as Desiree or Charlotte), peeled

½ onion, sliced

2 tbsp grated Pecorino Romano

50g breadcrumbs

2 sprigs of rosemary

Preheat the oven to 200°C/Gas 6. Grease a ceramic dish or deep roasting tray with olive oil.

Place the tomatoes in the tray, cut-side down, then lay the lamb cutlets on top and season with salt.

Cut the potatoes into slices about 3–4mm thick and place them in a layer over the lamb cutlets. Make sure the cutlets are completely covered, as this will ensure they are well cooked.

Scatter over the onion, Pecorino and breadcrumbs. Sprinkle over some more salt and drizzle on some olive oil. Lay the 2 rosemary sticks on top and place the tray in the oven for about 40 minutes, or until the potatoes are tender. Serve warm.

Mamma says

You can also try splashing a little white wine over the lamb cutlets before covering them with the layer of potatoes.

Bread and Pizza

It would be inconceivable not to have bread on our table, because if pasta is the queen of Puglian cuisine, then bread is certainly the king. My grandfather used to eat almost half a kilo a day, and he didn't like to see even a crumb of it thrown away, as it was 'a great sin before the Lord'. If it fell on the floor, you were supposed to pick it up and eat it.

The same applied to stale bread: it should not be wasted. The peasant families of Puglia always had to find ways to make use of it. Stale bread was grated or crushed into breadcrumbs, or was dunked in milk for breakfast. Some dipped it in red wine and seasoned it with salt, pepper and olive oil, while others ate it with their soups or baked it in the oven to make it crisp again.

The soft part of the bread could be fried and topped with anchovy to create a typical meal for Maundy Thursday. Or it could be used as baby food: soaked in warm water with sugar and olive oil, it would be given to babies between milk feeds.

I often look back to traditional dishes such as *bruschetta* and *crostini* to find inspiration, sometimes creating something new out of the old. Pizza and focaccia are also great, being both yeasty-light and easy to prepare. We often make pizza and focaccia together as a family at the weekend or during the holidays.

When we are in Puglia, we usually join ten or so other couples and their children and visit a friend with a wood-fired oven in the garden. We buy lots of small balls of dough from a nearby bakery and then get the children to roll them out for pizza bases. The toppings are all laid out on a table, and they decide what they want and put it on themselves – with some supervision, of course. Then the pizza goes in the outdoor oven to cook. There's a sense of sharing and community, with everyone involved: the children get their noses smudged with flour and it's big fun. That's how we spend summer evenings in the countryside.

Tomato and olive focaccia

Focaccia pugliex

Makes: 2 loaves
Prep: 20 mins (plus
   potato cooking time
   and rising time)
Cooking: 20 mins

My grandmother used to say that our cuisine holds *i raggi del sole*, the rays of the sun, and that focaccia represents our Puglian sun – perhaps because of the round shape suggested by its vernacular name of *cucchele*, circle.

If you visit Puglia, you'll find focaccia in every bakery. At noon each day, people queue up to buy a slice before wandering off to the Corso or the port for a walk or an *aperitivo*.

Being light and easy to digest, focaccia is ideal as a snack, a quick lunch or an evening bite with friends and their children.

300g floury or all-
   purpose potatoes
   (such as King Edward
   or Maris Piper)
1kg '00' white flour,
   plus extra for dusting
25g instant dried yeast
1 tsp caster sugar
2 tbsp fine salt
200ml olive oil
2 ripe vine tomatoes
Green olives, stone in
Sea salt
1 tsp oregano

Boil the potatoes until tender, then drain and leave to cool slightly. Peel and mash.

Pile the flour in a mound on a clean work surface (a large wooden board works best), or put it in a mixing bowl. Make a large well in the middle and place the mashed potatoes in it. Mix well.

In a bowl, dissolve the yeast in 250ml lukewarm water. Add the sugar.

Pour 200ml boiling water into a separate bowl. Stir in the salt.

Now make the dough. Gradually add first the yeast-water, then the salt-water, mixing with your hands until you get a smooth and slightly sticky ball of dough. Add a little more water if necessary.

Dust a little flour on the work surface and, if you mixed the dough in a bowl, transfer it to the work surface now. Knead the dough by pushing it out, folding it back, pushing it out and folding it back again a few times with the bottom of your palms. Turning the dough 90 degrees each time, repeat the push-fold-push-fold movement for 5-7 minutes (scrape in any residual dough from the work surface as you knead). You want a soft, sticky dough.

Place the dough in a large bowl. Dust some flour on top and cover the bowl with a damp tea towel, making sure there's lots of rising space. Leave to rise for 2 hours, or until doubled in size.

Preheat the oven to 220°C/Gas 7. Grease the bases of 2 non-stick tart tins (30cm in diameter) with 100ml olive oil each.

Divide the dough in half and spread to cover the whole base of each tin – use any oil that spills over to glaze the surface of the dough.

Roughly chop the tomatoes and rub the pieces across the focaccia, spreading out their juice.

Push the tomato pieces into the surface of the focaccia, along with the olives. Season the focaccia with sea salt and oregano.

Place the tins in the oven for 20 minutes, until the top of the focaccia turns golden-brown. Serve hot and crunchy.

Mozzarella crostini

Crostini con mozzarella

Makes: 4 slices
Prep: 5 mins
Cooking: 20 mins

Olive oil
Milk
4 slices of sourdough
   bread
1 x mozzarella (125g)
1 egg
30g grated Parmesan
Fine salt

These *crostini* can be regarded as the Italian version of Welsh rarebit, and they are usually eaten as an *antipasto* or a snack.

Preheat the oven to 180°/Gas 4. Grease a baking tray with olive oil.

Put some milk in a bowl – enough for dipping all of the sourdough slices into.

Submerge each slice of bread briefly in the milk, squeezing out any excess moisture. Lay the bread out on the greased tray and discard the remaining milk. Set the empty bowl aside.

Chop up the mozzarella and put it in the bowl. Crack the egg into the bowl, together with the Parmesan and a pinch of salt. Mix, then spoon the mixture onto the slices of bread.

Place the tray in the oven for about 20 minutes, until the mozzarella has turned slightly brown. Serve immediately.

Mamma says

If you prefer a lighter version, do not add the egg. For extra flavour, you can add a washed and desalted anchovy fillet or a slice of Parma ham on each crostino a couple of minutes before taking them out of the oven.

Tomato bruschetta

Bruschetta al pomodoro

Makes: 2 slices
Prep & cooking: 5 mins

Most Italian restaurants in Britain have their own version of this *antipasto* – but I recommend the original one, with a simple topping of chopped tomatoes. In Puglia we use bread from Altamura, near Bari, which is made with durum-wheat flour, to make this dish. Baked in wood-fired ovens, it can last up to two weeks thanks to its low water content. It is now sold in some delicatessens and pizzerias over here, but if you can't find it, use sourdough bread instead.

Beware of using too much garlic in this recipe! Garlic is not easy to digest, although my grandmother used to eat it raw – yes, raw – every single morning. She said it was good for her heart. She lived to a ripe old age, but it was challenging to have long face-to-face conversations with her.

2 slices of Altamura
  bread or sourdough
1 garlic clove, halved
About 6 cherry
  tomatoes
Sea salt
Olive oil

Toast or grill the slices of bread on both sides until you get a crunchy, golden-brown surface.

Rub one side of each slice with a halved garlic clove while the toast is still hot. Don't brush it too hard or more than once, otherwise it will be too garlicky. Discard the garlic halves.

If the bread is a bit stale or hard, brush each slice with the juicy side of a couple of halved cherry tomatoes to soften the surface. Allowing 2–3 tomatoes for each *bruschetta*, chop the cherry tomatoes into quarters. Place them on the slices of bread.

Add a pinch of salt and drizzle some olive oil on top – not too much. Serve while the *bruschette* are still warm.

Mamma says

When it comes to *bruschetta*, beware of complicated preparations: don't over-engineer this dish, keep it simple. In the Rome area, where my husband Alessandro comes from, they don't even add a topping of chopped tomatoes – and their *bruschetta* is just as delicious.

Puff pastry pizza

Pizza rustica

Serves: 4–6
Prep: 10 mins
Cooking: 40 mins

For years I ate this dish only at my mother's, as I was terrified of having to go through the lengthy and laborious process of making puff pastry. Then, one day, a friend of mine shook me by the shoulder and said: '*Ma che dici?* You can buy frozen puff pastry from any supermarket.' I was initially suspicious, but then I had to admit that it was just as good as my mamma's homemade pastry (good job she's not reading this), and the result was sensational.

Pizza rustica is a simple, traditional dish that has equivalents in other regions of Italy and across Europe; I particularly like my mamma's lighter version with ricotta, mozzarella and Italian cooked ham. It's ideal for birthday parties, picnics and other special occasions.

500g frozen puff pastry
Olive oil
Flour, for dusting
4 eggs
200g ricotta
40g sliced Italian
  cooked ham,
  shredded
2 x mozzarelle (250g),
  diced
Fine salt

Remove the pastry from the pack and leave to defrost for about 2–3 hours at room temperature.

Preheat the oven to 190°C/Gas 5. Grease the base and sides of a 30 x 20cm ceramic baking dish with olive oil.

Roll out half the pastry on a lightly floured work surface, until it's approximately 3–4mm thick. Carefully lay the pastry sheet out in the dish and prick it all over with a fork.

Crack the eggs, separating the yolks from the whites: pour the whites into a glass and tip the yolks into a bowl. Add the ricotta, ham and mozzarella cubes to the egg yolks. Mix well, then season with salt.

With the help of a spoon, spread the mixture across the whole surface of the pastry sheet.

Roll out the second pastry sheet and cut it into long strips. Place them over the filling layer, creating a grid or lattice pattern with a border round the edge.

Trim any excess dough hanging over the sides.

Brush the pastry grid or lattice with egg white. Put the dish in the preheated oven for about 40 minutes, until the crust turns golden-brown. Leave to cool before serving.

Mamma says

For vegetarian *pizza rustica*, make a ricotta and spinach filling. Start by preparing the pastry as usual.

Next, boil 400g spinach leaves in a little water, drain carefully and sauté in butter in a frying pan for a few minutes. Leave to cool.

Cut the sautéed spinach into small shreds and add them to a bowl containing 300g ricotta, 30g freshly grated Parmesan, 2 egg yolks, some salt and 1 teaspoon ground nutmeg for extra flavour, then mix well. Finish the *pizza rustica* as normal.

Alessandro's pizza

La pizza di Alessandro

Makes: 4 pizzas
Prep: 15 mins
 (plus rising time)
Cooking: 10–12 mins
 (plus rising time)

Making pizza over the weekend is something of a tradition in our family. As soon as the word 'pizza' is uttered, I bow out and leave the kitchen to my husband Alessandro, *il mago della pizza* ('the pizza wizard') – although I am no mean *pizzaiola* myself, I have to say.

Our children fight and vie to be Alessandro's sub-chefs. They love to roll the dough, choose the toppings and invent new shapes; flowers, butterflies, fish and owls have all made their appearance on the table at one time or another.

Pizza parties with school friends are always a great success too – there's no better way to keep children busy than getting them to bake their own pizza from scratch.

For the pizza dough
10g instant dried yeast
1 tsp caster sugar
500g '00' white flour,
 plus extra for dusting
1½ tsp fine salt
Olive oil

Toppings listed overleaf

Dissolve the yeast in a bowl containing 300ml lukewarm water, then stir in the sugar.

Pile the flour in a mound on a clean work surface (traditionally a large wooden board, which works best), or put it in a mixing bowl. Sprinkle on the salt, then make a large well in the centre of the pile. Pour a little bit of the yeast-water into the well and, with your hands, start bringing the flour mixture together from the outside towards the centre of the well. Adding more yeast-water as you go along, mix all the flour into a soft dough.

Dust a little flour on your work surface or board and knead the dough by pushing it out, folding it back, pushing it out and folding it back again a few times with the bottom of your palms. Turning the dough 90 degrees each time, repeat the push-fold-push-fold movement for 7–8 minutes, until you get a smooth, elastic ball of dough. While you knead, dust a little flour on the work surface, and scrape in any residual dough as you go.

Place the dough in a large bowl, then dust a little flour on top. Cover the bowl with a damp tea towel, making sure it doesn't touch the dough and there's plenty of rising space. Leave the dough to rise for 2 hours, or until roughly doubled in size.

When the dough is ready, preheat the oven to 220°C/Gas 7 and grease a pizza tray (or large baking tray) with olive oil.

Next, dust some flour on the work surface.

Take a lump of dough (about a quarter of the whole quantity) and roll it into a ball. Flatten it with your hand and roll it out from back to front and then back again with a rolling pin. Then lift the dough from the board, flip it, and turn it 90 degrees. Repeat the rolling movement (back-front-back-flip-turn) until you obtain a round pizza base about 2–3mm thick, stretching the dough with your hands now and then. If necessary, dust on a little flour after flipping, but be careful not to make the dough too dry.

Continues overleaf

For each margherita
  pizza
20ml passata
½ x mozzarella (65g),
  diced
Olive oil
Fine salt
2 tbsp black olives
  (optional)
3–4 basil leaves
  (optional)

For each potato and
  rosemary pizza
400g potatoes (any
  type), peeled
½ onion, finely sliced
Olive oil
2 sprigs of rosemary,
  picked over
Rock salt

For each frankfurter
  pizza
20ml passata
½ x mozzarella (75g),
  diced
2 frankfurters, sliced
Olive oil
Fine salt

Lay out the pizza base on the greased tray, and prick it all over with a fork. Now you can start covering the base as you wish – I have given just a few ideas below.

For a margherita pizza: Using a spoon, spread a thin layer of passata over the base. Make sure you don't apply it along the edges and that you don't drown the pizza in passata; you should still be able to see the white of the dough through the tomato sauce. Scatter the diced mozzarella on top. Drizzle over some olive oil and sprinkle on a pinch of salt. Black olives and basil can also be added, if you like.

For a potato and rosemary pizza: Cut the potatoes into very thin slices – up to 1mm thick – and spread them over the base, along with the onion. Season with olive oil, rosemary and rock salt.

For a frankfurter pizza: Spread a thin layer of passata over the base with a spoon (don't cover the edges with passata and keep the passata layer thin, so that you can still see the white of the dough through it). Scatter over the diced mozzarella and sliced frankfurters. Add a little olive oil and a pinch of fine salt.

Place the first pizza in the preheated oven for about 10 minutes. While it is cooking, roll out the next lump of dough and pick the pizza topping, continuing until all the pizzas are ready to eat.

Mamma says

If you are in a hurry and you can't wait two hours for the dough to rise, just put the bowl with the kneaded dough, covered with a damp tea towel, in a preheated oven at 45–50°C for 20 minutes. Your dough will then be ready for use.

If you make more dough than you need, you can always roll it into balls, wrap them in foil and put them in the freezer. The day you intend to use the dough, take the balls out of the freezer and put them on a plate at room temperature around three hours before you start the pizza making.

Snacks and Party Food

Parties are one of the greatest challenges for parents these days. Not only do they have to please their own children, but they must also try to outshine in quality, originality and sheer grandeur all the other parents' efforts. A great emphasis is put on the entertainment, while the food element is often neglected. When Eleonora and Emiliano come back from parties with their bags full of jelly gums and sugary cakes my heart sinks. 'Let me guess what you ate today,' I say with a sigh; 'soggy chips, microwaved pizza and chicken nuggets.' A guilty nod from the culprits.

This is all the more infuriating as making healthy, light and original party food does not require such a big effort. On the contrary, children can help cook the food themselves, which makes their day feel even more special – it brings them a sense of pride and helps boost self-confidence if they're able to give their own party a touch of individuality!

In the pages that follow, you will find simple recipes for party food and snacks which will help free you from the ubiquitous factory-produced packets of crisps and chocolate bars. Other recipes can work well at a party too, so do have a flick through the Bread and Pizza and Sweet Things chapters in particular; there are also some good options in the Pasta and Vegetable chapters.

Presentation is, of course, as important as the quality of the food that you're serving to your children's friends – and again it is fun to involve your children in writing the menus, setting the table, decorating the room and preparing the party bags (perhaps with a couple of recipes that your guests can take home to try). Forward thinking is key, and a little bit of planning will make an otherwise stressful occasion into a day to remember...

Fennel seed ring-biscuits

Taralli scaldati al finocchio

Serves: Makes about 50 savoury biscuits
Prep: 40 mins
Cooking: 40 mins (plus resting time)

Taralli are ring-shaped, savoury biscuit snacks that can be found in all good bakeries in Molfetta. The most common types are the plain ones or those flavoured with fennel seeds, but there are other versions too: with black pepper, tomato, oregano, paprika or crushed red chillies.

As well as making an excellent appetiser to accompany a glass of wine before dinner, *taralli* are a perfect snack for children: once they get a taste of them, they will no longer crave that packet of crisps. They are also ideal for toddlers with teething problems – much more effective than a dummy. In other words, *taralli* are loved by people of all ages and are totally addictive.

I usually make *taralli* at the weekend, with the children helping to shape the dough into rings. Kneading the dough for 20 minutes can be tiring, but it's a fantastic stress-relief exercise.

500g '00' white flour
100ml olive oil
100ml white wine
½ tsp fine salt
2 tbsp fennel seeds

Pile the flour in a mound on a clean work surface (traditionally a large wooden board, which works best), or put it in a mixing bowl. Make a large well in the middle with your fingers and fill it with the olive oil, wine, salt and fennel seeds. Using your hands, gradually incorporate the ingredients until everything is well combined, adding a bit of water (about 50–80ml) as you go along.

Dust a little flour on your work surface/board, and knead the dough by pushing it out, folding it back, pushing it out, then folding it back again with the bottom of your palm. Turning it 90 degrees, repeat the push-fold-push-fold movement for 20 minutes, until the dough is soft, smooth and lump-free. (It is not advisable to use a mixer.)

Now take a little piece of dough (about 15g) and roll it first between your hands and then on the work surface to create a long tube 12–15cm long and about 1cm thick. Shape it into an elongated ring and seal the edges by applying pressure with your thumb (in Molfetta everyone uses the tip of a key – 'This way,' they say, 'it'll never open up.'). As you create more *taralli* rings – all about the same size – place them on a clean and dry tea towel.

Continues overleaf

Once all the dough has been used, bring a deep, tall pan of water to the boil and pour cold tap water into a separate bowl.

Put no more than 6 *taralli* rings at one time in the boiling water. When they bob to the surface, use a skimmer to fish them out and dip them briefly into the cold-water bowl before placing them on a tea towel to dry and cool. When you are boiling the *taralli*, try not to drop them on top of one another, as they may stick together – if they do, use a spoon to separate them. Repeat the procedure until you have boiled all the rings.

Now go and have a couple of glasses of wine and come back 3 hours later. This will give the *taralli* enough time to dry out.

Preheat the oven to 200°C/Gas 6 and line some baking trays with baking parchment. Lay out the *taralli* on the parchment and put the trays in the oven for about 20–25 minutes, or until the *taralli* turn golden.

Remove the trays from the oven and leave the *taralli* to completely cool on racks. Eat them on the same day, or store in a sealed jar to keep them crisp and crunchy.

Spinach and ricotta frittata

Frittata di spinaci e ricotta

Serves: 4–6
Prep: 15 mins
Cooking: 30 mins

Despite its name, which derives from the word *fritto* ('fried'), this spinach and ricotta frittata is in fact an oven-baked dish that can be served either as a main course or as an *antipasto*. Ideal for parties, picnics and packed lunches, it's a recipe packed full of flavour, combining the slight bitterness of spinach with the delicate milky taste of ricotta.

All mothers should be grateful to Popeye, the cartoon character who gets his strength from spinach, for instilling in children a love of this healthy vegetable. He certainly had a positive impact on our children, and every time Emiliano eats this dish he swaggers around the house showing off his growing biceps.

Use fresh spinach rather than frozen: it has an infinitely better texture and flavour. The frittata can be stored for 2–3 days in the fridge, but make sure it's kept in an airtight container.

500g fresh spinach
120g (1 medium) leek, cleaned
Olive oil
½ onion, finely sliced
5 eggs
Fine salt
30g grated Parmesan
250g ricotta
Butter, for greasing

Preheat the oven to 180°C/Gas 4. Grease the base of a 23 x 20cm baking dish (at least 5cm deep) with butter.

Wash the spinach leaves well and boil them for a few minutes in a little water in a saucepan. Drain, squeezing out all the water until the spinach is fairly dry. Chop it finely and set it aside on a plate.

Meanwhile, chop off the root and the green part of the leek, and discard them. Cut the white part into thin slices and heat for a few minutes in a pan with 2 tablespoons of olive oil and the onion.

Crack and whisk the eggs in a bowl. Add a pinch of salt and the grated Parmesan. Tip the ricotta, spinach and the leek and onion mixture into the bowl and mix all the ingredients well.

Place the mixture in the greased dish and use a spoon to spread it out so it covers the whole base. Cook in the preheated oven for about 30 minutes, or until the frittata has set. Serve either warm or cold.

Asparagus frittata

Frittata di asparagi

Serves: 4
Prep: 5 mins
Cooking: 30 mins

'Look at your face – you could really do with a beaten egg!' my mamma would say when I came back from school looking tired. And before I could say a word, she'd beat one or two egg yolks in a bowl with some sugar and a bit of coffee – it kept me going like a train until dinnertime. Better than vitamins and supplements!

Children tend to love the flavour of eggs, and frittatas are a great way to introduce them to new vegetables. Spinach, courgettes, mushrooms, artichokes and courgette flowers are only some of the ingredients that can be included in this wonderfully versatile dish. The version below uses fine asparagus, chopped thinly, as some children can be fussy when they see 'green bits' in the frittata.

200g fine asparagus
5 eggs
20g grated Parmesan
3 sprigs of flat parsley
 leaves, chopped
Fine salt
Olive oil

Cut off and discard the woody parts of the asparagus. Boil the asaparagus in salted water for about 10 minutes. Drain and leave to cool, then slice finely and put aside.

In a bowl, crack and whisk the eggs. Add the Parmesan, chopped parsley and some salt. Heat up a little olive oil in a non-stick frying pan (26cm in diameter) and sauté the asparagus for a minute or so, but no more.

Pour in the beaten eggs and mix with the asparagus, then put a flat lid on the pan. Cook for 9–10 minutes over a medium heat, gently shaking the pan backwards and forwards from time to time to prevent the eggs from sticking to the bottom.

At that point, lift the pan from the heat and, pressing the lid firmly into place, turn the pan upside down, making sure the lid remains sealed. The frittata is now lying on the flat surface of your lid. Place the pan back on the heat and let the frittata slide gently back into the pan. Cook for another 5–6 minutes without the lid. Serve warm or cold.

Arancini with mozzarella and mince

Arancini

Makes: 16 large arancini
(or 32 small ones)
Prep: 30 mins
Cooking: 30 mins

These are rice-based snacks served in every rotisserie and take-away pizzeria in southern Italy. They can have different fillings and vary in size and appearance. The most common type is orange-shaped – hence the name *arancini* (little oranges).

Arancini are easy to make, but they require a long preparation time. I tend to make them over a weekend evening, after having had saffron risotto for lunch: by the time you start making the *arancini*, the leftover rice will have the perfect texture.

For the saffron risotto
½ vegetable stock cube
30g unsalted butter
Olive oil
½ onion, finely
  chopped
500g carnaroli or
  Arborio rice
½–1 tsp saffron strands
50g grated Parmesan

For the arancini
Olive oil
½ onion, finely sliced
150g lean beef mince
50ml red wine
100ml passata
Fine salt
Black pepper
80g petits pois
1 x mozzarella (125g)
2 eggs
100g breadcrumbs
50g white flour
Sunflower oil, for
  deep-frying

First make the risotto. In a saucepan bring 1½ litres of water to the boil and add the half vegetable stock cube.

In a separate saucepan, heat up the butter and 1 tablespoon of olive oil over a medium heat. Sauté the onion until it is translucent.

Add the rice and stir for a couple of minutes. Pour on a ladleful of stock and stir while the rice absorbs the liquid. Add the saffron (high-quality saffron is stronger so you'll need less of it) and Parmesan to the rice. Keep stirring all the time and gradually add stock as each ladleful of liquid is absorbed by the rice. After about 18 minutes, or when the rice is cooked and creamy, take off the heat and leave the risotto to cool. Set in the fridge for a few hours.

Next, make the filling for the arancini. Heat some olive oil in a saucepan over a medium heat. Sauté the onion until it becomes translucent. Add the mince and stir for a few minutes, then pour over the red wine.

At this point, add the passata and season with salt and pepper. Leave to simmer gently for about 15 minutes.

Meanwhile, in another saucepan, heat up 1 tablespoon more olive oil over a low heat and sauté the peas for about 10 minutes, or until cooked through. Add them to the beef and mix well.

Now cut the mozzarella into little cubes.

Next, spread the saffron risotto out on a flat plate. With wet hands, take some of the risotto and place it in your palm. Cup your hand and push the rice in so as to create a mould for the filling.

Put some pea-meat mixture in the mould and add one or two mozzarella cubes, then take some more rice with the other hand and seal the *arancino*, squeezing it into a round shape. Wetting your hands each time, proceed to the next one, until all the risotto has been used. (You can either choose to make about 16 large *arancini*, or 32 smaller ones.) Set the *arancini* aside.

Beat the eggs in a shallow bowl and spread the breadcrumbs on a plate. Spread the flour on another plate. One by one, roll the *arancini* in the flour, then in the beaten egg, and finally in the breadcrumbs.

Pour enough sunflower oil into a deep saucepan to fill it by no more than a third. Heat the oil to a deep-frying temperature – for larger *arancini*, this is best at 170°C (when a cube of bread turns brown in 1 minute 15 seconds) and for smaller ones this is best at 180°C (when a cube of bread turns brown in about 1 minute); turn down the heat slightly if the oil gets too hot. Fry the arancini, no more than two at a time if large, or four at a time if small, until golden-brown, carefully turning them over in the oil so they brown all over, then drain them in a bowl lined with kitchen paper. Allow the oil to re-heat between batches.

Serve while still hot, allowing 2 large *arancini* per person, or else 4 small ones.

Mamma says

Arancini are just what you need for your party table, and they can be served either as an appetiser or as a main. You can make them well in advance, keep them in the fridge and fry them when you want them. As a matter of fact, they are even tastier and hold together better if they're left to sit for a few hours before being fried.

As an alternative, you can fill the *arancini* with mozzarella cubes and shreds of Italian cooked ham, rather than with mince and peas.

Potato croquettes
Crocchette di patate

Serves: 4
Prep: 20 mins (plus
  potato cooking time)
Cooking: 20 mins

Crocchette di patate are great for parties, picnics and packed lunches. They don't lose any of their tastiness the next day and – needless to say – children adore them. The other day I had to stop Emiliano, who had stealthily infiltrated the kitchen, from eating his fifth croquette in a row.

Made of mashed potatoes, the croquettes are usually filled with mozzarella cubes and shreds of Italian cooked ham. My mamma uses smoked *scamorza* (a cheese similar to mozzarella, but firmer and saltier), which can also be found in this country.

500g floury or all-
  purpose potatoes
  (such as King Edward
  or Maris Piper)
2 knobs of unsalted
  butter
Fine salt
1 egg
50g grated Parmesan
Flour or breadcrumbs
  (if needed)
Sunflower oil, for
  deep-frying

For the coating
2 eggs
100g white flour
100g breadcrumbs

For the filling
100g smoked
  scamorza (or
  mozzarella)
60g sliced Italian
  cooked ham

Boil the potatoes in abundant water for about 20–25 minutes until they are tender. Drain them in a colander and leave to cool, then peel and mash into a purée with a fork.

Melt the butter in a frying pan over a low heat. Add the potato purée to the pan and cook for a few minutes – stir with a wooden spoon so that it becomes smooth and compact. Add some salt.

Tip the potato purée into a bowl. Crack the egg into the purée, add the Parmesan and mix well. If the potato mixture is too soft, add a tablespoon or more of flour (or breadcrumbs).

Now crack the eggs for the coating into another bowl, and whisk. Tip the flour onto one plate and the breadcrumbs onto a second plate.

Next make the filling: dice the scamorza (or mozzarella) and shred the ham.

Take a walnut-sized piece of potato mixture and with your finger create a hole, then fill with a couple of cheese cubes and some ham. Cover the hole and with your hands roll the mixture into a cylinder. You can make larger or smaller croquettes, as you like.

At this point, roll the mixture in the flour, shaking off any excess, then coat it in beaten egg and then breadcrumbs. Repeat the process of making croquettes until all the mixture has been used.

Pour enough sunflower oil into a deep saucepan to fill it by no more than a third. Heat the oil to a deep-frying temperature (180°C, or until a cube of bread goes brown in about 1 minute; turn down the heat slightly if the oil gets too hot). Fry the croquettes, no more than 2–3 at a time, for about 2 minutes, until they turn golden-brown on all sides, then drain them in a bowl lined with kitchen paper. Allow the oil to re-heat between batches.

Serve the croquettes hot.

Mamma says

For extra flavour, try adding 1–2 teaspoons of ground nutmeg to the potato mixture before filling and shaping the croquettes.

Stuffed deep-fried parcels
Frittelle

Makes: about 24 frittelle
Prep & cooking:
  45 mins–1 hour
  (plus rising time)

These savoury pastries are to Puglian cuisine what pizza is to Neapolitan. Tradition demands that they should be prepared on 11 November, St Martin's Day, to celebrate the *estate di San Martino* (Indian summer). *Frittelle* can be deep-fried or oven-baked and although the latter is a healthier option, I still prefer the fully loaded version – as you can tell, I am a real *frittelle* junkie.

This is the ideal recipe for any kind of party or festivity. If you're having an informal dinner with friends, you can serve the *frittelle* with salami and cheese.

For the dough
150g floury or all-
  purpose potatoes
  (such as King Edward
  or Maris Piper)
500g '00' white flour,
  plus extra for dusting
12g instant dried yeast
½ tsp caster sugar
1 tbsp fine salt
Sunflower oil,
  for deep-frying

For the ricotta and
  ham filling
1 egg
200g ricotta
1 tbsp grated Parmesan
60g sliced Italian
cooked ham, shredded
Fine salt

Continues opposite

To make the dough, follow the method for focaccia on page 152, dissolving the yeast in 125ml water and the salt in 100ml water.

While the dough is rising, make the fillings. First make the ricotta and ham filling. Crack and whisk the egg in a bowl, then mix in the ricotta, Parmesan, ham and a pinch of salt.

Next make the cheese and tomato filling. Mix the mozzarella, tomatoes, Parmesan, oregano and a pinch of salt. Place on a plate, or in a sieve, discarding any excess liquid.

When the dough is ready, make 24 small balls of about 40g each and place them on the work surface (traditionally a wooden board), dusting it with flour if your dough is sticky.

To fill the *frittelle*, roll out each small ball to create a circle about 10-12cm in diameter and 2mm thick. For half of the *frittelle*, spoon into the middle just under 1 tablespoon of the cheese and tomato filling (the filling must be thoroughly drained, otherwise it might spill out when frying, causing the oil in the pan to spit). For the rest of the *frittelle*, spoon in just over 1 tablespoon of the ricotta and ham filling.

Fold each circle in half; seal the edges first with your thumb and then with the prongs of a fork. Make sure you have pushed out all the air, otherwise the *frittelle* may open while you are frying them.

For the cheese and tomato filling

1 x mozzarella (125g), diced

50g tinned plum tomatoes, chopped and juices drained

2 tbsp grated Parmesan

1 tsp dried oregano

Fine salt

Pour enough sunflower oil into a deep saucepan to fill it by no more than a third. Heat the oil to a deep-frying temperature (180°C, or when a cube of bread goes brown in about 1 minute; turn down the heat if the oil gets too hot). One by one (or 2–3 at a time in a larger pan) fry the *frittelle* until golden-brown, 1–2 minutes each side. Remove and drain on a plate lined with kitchen paper. Allow the oil to re-heat between batches and serve the *frittelle* while still hot.

Mamma says

When eating *frittelle* 'out of the pan', be careful not to scorch your palate (which I inevitably do each time) on the very hot filling.

If you're feeling adventurous, try fillings such as tuna and capers, or salted anchovies and peeled plum tomatoes.

Sweet Things

$N\!ot$ too far away from my family home, there was a lady who used to prepare the most delicious traditional sweets every Christmas. My mamma was one of her loyal customers, and would pay her an annual visit in mid-December to buy some homemade pastries. I needed no prodding to accompany her and liked to have my say on the choice of sweets for our table.

For a sweet-toothed child such as myself, entering the lady's house was like stepping into Aladdin's cave. There were baking trays of pastry lying everywhere to cool – on tables, on sofas, on sideboards, on beds – and once I inadvertently fulfilled one of my earliest fantasies by tripping on a tray on the floor and diving face first into a fragrant array of just-baked tartlets and pies. My mother was all apologies, but the lady, rather than scolding me, offered me a *canestrello di cioccolato e mandorle* (chocolate almond bite) to taste. The smell of that house and the flavour of that *canestrello* are still vivid in my memory, as is the bump on my head.

Until after the Second World War, sugar was considered a luxury in Puglia, so sweets were only eaten during festivities. There are different pastries according to the time of the year and the seasonal ingredients available – with one constant, however: almonds.

Almond trees are a familiar sight in our countryside, and in the spring their white and pink flowers colour vast swathes of the Puglian landscape. Milk and oil produced from almonds have been used for centuries in our region as natural remedies to cure sore throats, coughs and stomach aches. I am sure there must be some aphrodisiac based on almonds too. Until not too long ago it was common to see, on people's doorsteps, mounds of almonds drying in the sun. Things have changed in recent years, but almonds still remain one of the core ingredients of our cuisine.

In this chapter, I have decided to steer away from the ubiquitous tiramisù and panna cotta, or traditional pastries that are too much of an acquired taste (featuring ingredients such as honey, figs and vincotto, a dark syrupy wine made from local red grapes), and concentrate instead on the sweets and cakes that brightened my childhood and continue to give joy to our children and their friends.

Marzipan sweets with glacé cherries

Dolcetti al marzapane con ciliegia

Makes: 16–18 sweets
Prep: 20 minutes
Cooking: 15 mins

Marzipan sweets – made of ground almonds, eggs and sugar – are usually eaten around Christmas time in Puglia. I tend to make them throughout the year however, as our children refuse to wait until Christmas. They are a wonderful after-school snack, and great for afternoon teas and parties.

Peeled (or blanched) almonds are not hard to come by in groceries and supermarkets, but if you can't find them, raw almonds with skin will do: just place them in hot water (a little below boiling point) for five minutes to loosen their skin, then drain and leave them cool. With a gentle squeeze, they will slip out of their skins.

500g blanched
  almonds
Finely grated zest of
  1 lemon
1 tsp ground cinnamon
70g caster sugar
3 eggs, at room
  temperature
1 tsp vanilla extract
About 100g glacé
  cherries

Preheat the oven to 180°C/Gas 4.

Grind the almonds in a food processor, in small batches, until they are reduced to a fine powder and tip into a large bowl. Add the lemon zest to the almonds, together with the cinnamon.

Now add 30g of the sugar and mix well. Make a large well in the centre of the mixture and crack the eggs into it, then pour in the vanilla extract. Using your hands, mix well.

Spread the remaining 40g sugar across a plate. Take a piece of dough (about 35g) and roll it into a ball. Roll the ball in the sugar. Place it on a baking tray lined with baking parchment. Repeat the procedure until all the dough has been used. Remember to leave a little space between the sweets, because they expand in the oven.

Cut the glacé cherries in half and gently push one half-cherry into each dough ball, cut side down. Put the tray in the oven for about 15 minutes or until firm but turning pale brown. Leave the sweets to cool on the tray before serving.

Mamma says

If you're feeling lazy, use ground almonds instead of grinding whole blanched ones – you'll just lose a little bit of freshness.

Chocolate almond bites

Canestrelli di cioccolato e mandorle

Makes: 16 sweets
Prep & cooking:
 20 mins

On the morning of the sixth of December, St Nicholas' Day, Puglian children get their Christmas presents. When I was little, these were usually piled on the dining-room table and accompanied by a plate full of pastries and chocolate-and-almond snacks, adding to the excitement and pleasure of the occasion. Unfortunately the canestrelli didn't tend to last very long, because I found my brother – another sweet addict in the making – the fiercest of competitors.

My auntie is a real expert at making *canestrelli*, and I had always thought it would be hard for me to compete with her until a friend showed me a battered old little notebook scrawled with barely legible numbers and words. She said it belonged to her grandmother and contained much arcane lore about Puglian sweets, including the following elementary recipe.

350g blanched
 almonds
150g milk chocolate
150g dark chocolate

Preheat the oven to 180°C/Gas 4 and grease 16 cupcake moulds with butter.

Spread the almonds on a baking tray and put in the oven for 10 minutes, stirring them around a few times to ensure they toast evenly. They are ready when light brown; take care they do not go too dark or they will taste bitter. Leave the almonds to cool for a few minutes.

Wrap the almonds in a clean tea towel and, with the help of a rolling pin (or similar), crush them until they are reduced to fragments.

Break both chocolates into pieces, then place in a saucepan and melt on a low heat, stirring often. Take off the heat, then add the crushed almonds and mix well for a few minutes. Spoon the mixture into the cupcake moulds – about 2 tablespoons each. Leave to cool, then place in the fridge for an hour or so.

Serve the *canestrelli* in coloured cupcake cases.

Crispy ring-pastries

Taralli all'uovo

Makes: about
25 pastries
Prep: 15 mins
Cooking: 15–20 mins

Taralli all'uovo were the most delicious snacks that came from the oven of my grandmother, Nonna Lina. When we were little, my brother and I used to stay with her after school, and the highlight of the afternoon was when she would bring us a glass of milk and these crunchy pastries. They made homework an easier load to bear.

Since my nonna is no longer with us, I asked a *pasticceria* in Molfetta if they could give me their *taralli* recipe, and they have been kind enough to let me share it with you. Having now tried it many times at home, I can confidently say that the result is just as crispy and flavoursome as Nonna Lina's version.

500g '00' white flour
3 eggs, at room
    temperature
200g caster sugar
100g olive oil
1 tsp baking powder
1 tsp vanilla extract
Finely grated zest
    of 1 lemon

Preheat the oven to 160°C/Gas 3 and line a baking tray with baking parchment.

Place the flour in a mound on a work surface (traditionally a wooden board); you could also use a large mixing bowl. Make a large well in the centre and crack the eggs into it, then add the sugar, olive oil, baking powder, vanilla extract and lemon zest and mix.

On your work surface/board, knead the dough by pushing it out, folding it back, pushing it out, then folding it back again with the bottom of your palm. Then, turning it 90 degrees, repeat the same movement for 10 minutes until the dough has a smooth texture.

Take a piece of dough (about 30–40g) and roll it on your work surface to create a tube about 1cm thick. Loop the tube into a ring and seal the edges by pushing down with your finger. Repeat the procedure until all the dough has been used to make about 25 rings.

Place the rings on the lined tray, leaving a bit of space between them. Put the tray in the oven for 15–20 minutes until the *taralli* turn golden. Let them cool completely before serving as a snack.

Mamma says

The *taralli* can be stored for up to ten days in an air-tight container.

Angel wings

Chiacchiere

Serves: 4
Prep: 10 mins (plus
resting time)
Cooking: 20 mins

Angel wings are sweet crunchy pastries. In my region they are
called *chiacchiere*, which means 'gossip', whereas in Liguria they
are called *bugie*, or 'fibs'. Perhaps they are given such unflattering
names because they are just as easy to make and to eat as it is to
spread gossip or tell a lie.

Chiacchiere are traditionally made during Carnival, when our
streets are crowded with floats, parades and masked people. They
are as essential to Carnival as masks and confetti.

Try involving your children in the preparation of *chiacchiere*,
cutting the dough into strips or dusting on the icing sugar.

500g '00' white flour,
plus extra for dusting
1 tsp baking powder
1 tbsp caster sugar
3 eggs, at room
temperature
30g unsalted butter,
softened
200ml white wine
Sunflower oil, for
deep-frying
Icing sugar

In a large bowl, mix the flour, baking powder and sugar. Next add
1 whole egg, 2 egg yolks (save the whites for another use) and the
butter. Pour the wine into the bowl slowly, mixing with your hands.

Lift the dough onto a lightly floured work surface (a large wooden
board is traditional and works best). Knead it into a smooth ball,
slightly sticky to the touch. Wrap the dough in cling film and leave
to rest for half an hour.

Divide the dough into 3–4 pieces. Dust the work surface with flour,
roll out the first pastry piece to about 2mm thick and cut it into
rectangular strips (3–4cm by 10cm) with a pastry wheel or a knife.
Repeat with the rest of the dough.

Pour enough sunflower oil into a deep saucepan to fill it by no more
than a third. Heat it to 180°C (or until a cube of bread goes brown in
about 1 minute); turn down the heat slightly if the oil gets too hot.

Fry the *chiacchiere*, up to 4 at a time, until golden-brown. Remove
to a bowl lined with kitchen paper. Allow the oil to re-heat between
batches. Dust the fried *chiacchiere* with icing sugar and serve.

Mamma says

Any leftover *chiacchiere* will keep in a paper bag for up to two days.

Apricot crostata
Crostata all'albicocca

Serves: 8
Prep: 20 mins
  (plus resting time)
Cooking: 30–35 mins

Crostata is a classic Italian tart which has a jam or chocolate filling. The jam used for the traditional Puglian *crostata* is made from the pulp and skin of figs, which are common and abundant in our region in the summer. However, since fig jam is quite sweet and may not be to everyone's taste, I suggest opting for an apricot or peach preserve instead.

Because of its elegant appearance, *crostata* is ideal as a party cake for children or as a crunchy dessert to be served to your guests just before coffee.

300g '00' white flour
2 eggs, at room
  temperature
100g caster sugar
90g softened unsalted
  butter, plus extra for
  greasing
1 tsp baking powder
½ tsp vanilla extract
Finely grated zest of
  1 lemon
400g apricot or peach
  jam

Pile the flour in a small mound on your work surface (in Puglia this is traditionally a large wooden board, which works best); you can also use a large mixing bowl.

Make a well in the centre and crack 1 egg into it. Add the yolk of the second egg, reserving the white in a small bowl. Finally, mix the sugar, butter, baking powder, vanilla extract and lemon zest into the flour mixture to make a dough.

On your work surface/board, knead the dough by pushing it out, folding it back, pushing it out and folding it back again with the bottom of your palm, then turning it 90 degrees. Knead like this for 10 minutes until the dough achieves a smooth texture. Wrap the dough in cling film and leave it to rest in the fridge for 30 minutes.

Once the dough has rested, preheat the oven to 180°C/Gas 4.

Split the dough into 2 parts, one slightly bigger than the other, and roll out the larger part to a thickness of 2–3mm.

Now grease the base and the sides of a round tart tin (26-28cm in diameter) with butter. Place the rolled out dough in the tin (roll the dough around the pin and then unroll it in the tin) and spread it with your hands to cover the entire base. Prick it all over with a fork, then spoon the jam onto the base and spread it evenly to within 1cm of the edge.

Roll out the remaining dough to a thickness of 2–3mm. With the help of a pastry wheel or knife, cut it into strips about 2cm wide. Be careful when you lift the strips of dough, as they can easily break.

Form a lattice pattern with the strips above the layer of jam. Roll any residual dough into a long tube around 1cm thick and press it all around the edge to seal the *crostata*.

Brush the dough lattice with the reserved egg white. Bake for 30–35 minutes, until golden-brown. Leave to cool, then serve.

Mamma says

A *crostata* will keep in a paper bag or wrapped in foil for up to 4 days.

yoghurt cake
Torta allo yogurt

Serves: 8
Prep: 10 mins
Cooking: 30–35 mins

The yoghurt cake is also known in Italian as the 'seven pots cake', because the empty yoghurt pot is used as a measuring cup.

Our children love to make this cake on their own. I arrange all the ingredients on the table and leave the kitchen, telling them: 'Just make sure you don't put a pot of salt in it.' These days, this elicits rolling eyes rather than a laugh – they have heard that joke many times before.

When they have finished, I am summoned back in to put the cake in the oven. For tasting and eating it, however, they never require any assistance.

3 eggs, at room
  temperature
1 x 125g pot of peach
  yoghurt
1 yoghurt-pot measure
  of sunflower oil
2 yoghurt-pot measures
  of caster sugar
3 yoghurt-pot measures
  of '00' white flour
2 tsp baking powder
1 tsp vanilla extract
Fine salt
Icing sugar, to finish

Grease the base and the sides of a 23cm diameter cake tin with sunflower oil, and dust it with flour. Preheat the oven to 180°C/Gas 4.

Crack the eggs into a mixing bowl and stir to combine with the peach yoghurt. Now use the empty yoghurt pot as a measuring cup. Measure the sunflower oil, sugar and flour into the bowl. Add the baking powder, the vanilla extract and a pinch of fine salt. Mix until smooth.

Pour the mixture into the cake tin and put it in the oven for about 30–35 minutes, or until a skewer or cocktail stick slid into the centre of the cake comes out clean.

Leave the cake to cool, then dust with icing sugar before serving.

For preparing the tin
Sunflower oil
Flour

Mamma says

Once the cake has cooled, you could cut it in half and fill it with a layer of jam. Alternatively, top the cake with sliced peaches for dramatic effect, as shown opposite.

For extra flavour, include the zest of 1 lemon in the mixture along with the other ingredients.

Pastry cream dessert

Crema pasticcera

Serves: 6
Prep: 15 mins
Cooking: 10 mins

Pastry cream is generally used for filling cakes, but it can also be served on its own, hot or cold, dusted with cocoa powder. My grandmother used to make it most Sundays and serve it with fruit as the *coup de grâce* at the end of a long meal.

She would marinate chopped bananas, kiwis and strawberries in lemon juice and sugar for about half an hour, then put them in large cups, pour some pastry cream on top and leave them in the fridge for about two hours. Usually, my brother and I couldn't wait that long and would be caught cream-handed with our fingers in the cups.

Pastry cream is not difficult to make, but it requires some care, because if you don't keep stirring all the time while it's cooking, it can get too thick and lumpy.

This is a fantastic dessert for children, which requires only a few basic ingredients – eggs, sugar, flour and milk.

500ml milk
1 vanilla pod
6 egg yolks
150g sugar
50g '00' white flour

Pour 300ml of the milk into a saucepan, leaving the rest in a glass. Remove the seeds from the vanilla pod with the tip of a knife or a teaspoon and add them to the pan, together with the pod.

Bring the milk to the boil on a low heat, then take the pan off the heat and leave the vanilla pod to continue infusing in the milk for about 10 minutes.

Remove the vanilla pod from the pan. Using an electric hand mixer on low speed, combine the egg yolks and sugar in a bowl for about 1 minute, until you obtain a smooth mixture. As you mix, pour one third of the warm milk from the pan into the bowl. Continuing to mix, sift the flour into the bowl a little at a time.

Add the egg-and-flour mixture to the rest of the milk in the pan, then bring to the boil on a low heat, stirring constantly.

When the mixture starts getting thicker, add the reserved milk from the glass in a thin stream. Keep on stirring for a couple of minutes and then remove from the heat. Transfer to a bowl.

Cover the bowl with a clean, wet tea towel to prevent the formation of a skin on the surface.

If you are not planning to use the cream immediately, you can store it in the fridge for up to two days in a container covered with a damp tea towel, or with baking parchment or cling film directly applied to the cream's surface.

Take the cream out of the fridge 30 minutes before serving, whisk, and eat it at room temperature, with fruit alongside, if you like.

Mamma says

To add extra flavour, peel the zest of 1 lemon with a vegetable peeler or knife (avoiding the white pith) and add it with the vanilla pod to the milk. The lemon zest must be removed at the same time as the vanilla pod.

You can make your cream thicker or thinner by adding more flour or more milk as necessary.

Yo-yo cakes

Yo-yo

Makes: 6 yo-yos
Prep: 15 mins
Cooking: 15 mins

Who hasn't played with a yo-yo as a child – or even as a grown-up? If you want to give your children a real treat, or you're throwing a party for them and their friends, then yo-yo cakes are a must.

Most of my friends mould these cakes into the traditional macaroon shape, but I have decided to follow my mamma's recipe and give them a more fanciful butterfly or diabolo shape.

Yo-yo cakes are very easy to make, and if you think Nutella is too debauched, you can fill them with homemade jam or marmalade.

And before the party begins, why not get the children to help you decorate and personalise their own?

3 eggs, at room
  temperature
100g caster sugar
100g '00' white flour
8g or 2 tsp baking
  powder
About 50g Nutella
  (or jam)
Sweets, to decorate
  (optional)

Place 12 paper cupcake cases on a baking tray, then double them up with another 12 cases so that the cakes hold their shape better. Preheat the oven to 180°C/Gas 4.

Crack the eggs into a bowl. Add the sugar and flour and, with the help of an electric hand mixer, combine.

Mix in the baking powder.

Pour the mixture into the paper cases so they are two thirds full. When you have used all the mixture, put the baking tray in the oven for about 15 minutes, or until the cakes are risen and cooked through (a skewer or cocktail stick slid into the centre should come out clean).

Once the little cupcakes have cooled down, remove them from their cases. Now, with the help of a knife, make a hole (around 1cm deep) at the bottom of each cake and fill it with Nutella or jam.

To make one yo-yo, join two cakes together by their bases, using Nutella (or jam) as the 'cement'. Before serving the yo-yos, you can embellish them with decorations or add a liquorice string to each one.

Ring Cake

Ciambellone

Serves: 8
Prep: 15 mins
Cooking: 40 mins

This popular cake – which takes its name from its circular shape resembling a big *ciambella*, or doughnut – is made from simple ingredients, and can be served at breakfast with milk or enjoyed as an afternoon snack. With the right decorations, it can also turn into an inventive birthday cake.

Ciambellone is a fantastic alternative to industrially produced cakes and biscuits, and it's so easy to make that even young children and people who have never baked a cake in their life can have a go at it. Just make sure you have the right round-shaped baking mould before you start mixing the ingredients!

150g softened unsalted butter, plus extra for greasing
300g '00' white flour, plus extra for dusting
3 eggs
200g caster sugar
180ml milk
Finely grated zest of 1 lemon
Fine salt
1½ tsp baking powder
1 tsp vanilla extract
2 tbsp cocoa powder
Icing sugar, for dusting

Grease a ring baking mould (25cm in diameter and at least 5cm deep) with butter and then dust it with a little flour. Preheat the oven to 180°C/Gas 4.

Crack the eggs into a bowl and lightly whisk with an electric hand mixer.

Using the hand mixer, mix in the sugar. Do the same with the butter, flour, milk, lemon zest and a pinch of salt; the texture should be smooth and creamy. Mix in the baking powder and vanilla extract.

Place half of the mixture in the mould, spreading it evenly. Sift the cocoa powder into the remaining mixture and combine. Spread the chocolate mixture over the mixture already in the mould.

Put the mould in the oven and leave for about 40 minutes, until the cake has turned golden-brown. Check that it's cooked by piercing it with a skewer or cocktail stick. If it comes out sticky, just cook the cake for a little longer.

Leave to cool on a rack, then dust some icing sugar over and serve.

Mamma says

The *ciambellone* will keep for a few days in a cool place.

Ricotta and chocolate semifreddo cake

Zuccotto

Serves: 6
Prep: 30 mins
Cooking: 45 mins

Zuccotto is a *semifreddo* (or semi-frozen) dessert made with sponge cake, whipped cream and bits of chocolate. The name *zuccotto* means 'pumpkin', which is similar to its shape. Originally from Tuscany, it has become one of the most popular desserts in Puglia, where it is usually served at the end of a long Sunday nosh-up, particularly during the summer.

Traditionally, the sponge cake is soaked in brandy or limoncello. As a child-friendly alternative, I have used milky coffee in the version below. You can make the coffee using a Moka or other coffee machine, or alternatively, just use instant coffee.

To get the best result in terms of texture and taste, I suggest you prepare the *zuccotto* well in advance, keeping it in the freezer for at least 12 hours before serving.

For the sponge cake
Butter, for greasing
200g '00' white flour, plus extra for dusting
3 eggs, at room temperature
200g caster sugar
2 tbsp milk
1½ tsp baking powder
50ml strong coffee diluted with 100ml milk

First prepare the sponge cake. Grease the base and the sides of a cake tin (23cm in diameter) and dust it with some flour. Preheat the oven to 150°C/Gas 2.

Crack and whisk the eggs in a bowl and add the sugar. Using an electric hand mixer, mix the ingredients for 2–3 minutes.

Add the flour, milk and baking powder and mix until the texture is smooth and creamy.

Pour the mixture into the prepared cake tin and put it in the oven for 45 minutes, or until a cocktail stick or skewer poked into the centre comes out clean.

For the filling
250g whipping cream
150g icing sugar
600g ricotta
80g chocolate chips or beans
30g cocoa powder
Icing sugar, for dusting (optional)

Next, prepare the filling. Put the cream and icing sugar in a bowl and, with a hand whisk, whip the ingredients until soft peaks form.

Use a wooden spoon to push the ricotta through a medium-meshed sieve into the bowl – this will make it creamier. Mix together.

Pour half of the ricotta-cream mixture into a separate bowl. Add the chocolate chips (or beans) to the first bowl, and stir them in.

Sift the cocoa powder into the other bowl and mix until you get a smooth brown cream.

Finally, assemble the *zuccotto*. Line a dome-shaped cake mould or glass bowl (about 20cm in diameter) with cling film. Once the sponge cake has cooled down, slice off its top (around 3cm thick) and put it to one side. Take the remaining part and slice it into strips about 2cm wide.

Brush each strip with milky coffee and, working from the bottom up, place the strips horizontally in the mould or bowl to cover the entire inner surface. Don't worry if the strips break up; you can mould them back into shape with your hands.

Now pour the brown cream into the sponge-lined mould or bowl, followed by the white mixture with chocolate bits, then cover using the remaining part of the sponge cake as a lid.

Soak the sponge-cake lid with the remaining milky coffee. Cover with cling film.

Put the *zuccotto* in the freezer for at least 12 hours, to make it firm and give it a fine *semifreddo* texture.

About 4 hours before serving, turn the cake mould (or bowl) upside down onto a plate and remove the cling film. Leave it to defrost at room temperature for around 3½–4 hours, until the *zuccotto* filling achieves the same texture as soft ice cream. Dust the *zuccotto* with icing sugar, if you like, and serve in slices.

Mamma says

Any leftover *zuccotto* will keep in the fridge for 24 hours.

Chocolate-dipped shortbread

Frollini al cioccolato

Makes: 30 biscuits
Prep: 25 mins
Cooking: 20 mins

When I moved to England, one of the things I missed most were these delicious biscuits, which I used to buy from my favourite pastry shop in Molfetta. After years of pining, I decided to try my hand at making them and was surprised at how easy it was. Now *frollini* have become the children's staple after-school snack and a perfect accompaniment to my husband's very English cup of tea.

With the help of a piping bag, you and your children can design your own shape of biscuits. The most common ones are the ring, horseshoe and half-moon, but the one that I like most is the 'S' – a letter I sometimes feel should be stitched onto *my* T-shirt rather than Clark Kent's as I try to juggle work, house, kids and *frollini*-baking all at the same time.

250g unsalted butter, softened
150g icing sugar
3 eggs, at room temperature
Fine salt
Finely grated zest of 1 lemon
375g '00' white flour
About 40–60ml milk, if necessary
100g dark chocolate

Line a baking tray with baking parchment.

Combine the butter and icing sugar in a food processor for about 10 minutes. If you don't have a food processor, you can use a large bowl and an electric hand mixer instead.

As you keep mixing, add an egg, then a second one and then the yolk of a third one (you can save the extra white for another use). Make sure that each egg has been perfectly absorbed and combined before adding the next one.

Still mixing, add a pinch of salt and the lemon zest, then gradually sieve in the flour. Add some milk if needed, to get a creamy texture.

Transfer the mixture to a piping bag – a 10mm nozzle works well, but it's up to you! Pipe the mixture onto the lined tray to create your favourite biscuit shapes, leaving a bit of space between them.

Leave the tray in the fridge for an hour, then preheat the oven to 180°C/Gas 4.

Put the tray in the oven for about 15–20 minutes, or until the biscuits are slightly brown. Remove from the oven and leave to cool on a rack.

Meanwhile, melt the chocolate in a bain-marie: bring a pot of water to the boil, then set a heatproof bowl on top of the pan (without the base touching the water), put the chocolate in, and cover. When the chocolate has melted, put it aside to cool slightly.

Dip the biscuits in the melted chocolate. Put on a rack with a baking tray underneath; once the chocolate is solid, the biscuits are ready.

Mamma says

Take the butter and the eggs out of the fridge at least an hour before you start making the biscuits. The eggs must be at room temperature and the butter must be soft but not melted.

Chocolate 'salami'

Salame al cioccolato

Serves: 6–8
Prep: 30 mins
Setting: 3 hours

This recipe, which takes its name from the vague resemblance to a salami, was given to me by a friend who has a full-time job in a bank but loves cooking cakes and biscuits at the weekend.

It is easy to prepare and ideal for private parties and not-so-private guilty pleasures. And I find that children love helping to crush the biscuits and mix the ingredients.

If you're uncomfortable about giving your children raw eggs, you can just leave them out of the recipe. In that case the mixture will be harder to work – but the chocolate salami will be easier to digest.

200g dark chocolate
300g Rich Tea biscuits
 or digestives
100g caster sugar
150g unsalted butter,
 softened
2 eggs, at room
 temperature
Icing sugar, for dusting
Vanilla ice cream,
 to serve (optional)

Melt the chocolate in a bain-marie: bring a pot of water to the boil, then set a heatproof bowl on top of the pan (without the base touching the water), put the chocolate in, and cover. When the chocolate has melted, put it aside to cool slightly.

Meanwhile, place the biscuits on a wooden board with a clean tea towel on top and, with the help of a rolling pin (or similar), crush them until they are reduced to fragments.

In a bowl, mix the caster sugar with the butter using a spoon. Crack and whisk the eggs in a separate bowl, then pour them into the bowl. Add the melted chocolate and the crushed biscuits. Mix well.

Place the mixture in the middle of a sheet of baking parchment. Dust some icing sugar on top. Fold the paper over the mixture and mould it into a cylinder shape. Wrap the cylinder in foil, twist the ends to seal, and leave in the fridge for at least 3 hours.

The longer the chocolate salami can stay in the fridge the better. Once it has set, remove from the fridge, unwrap and serve sliced, on its own or with vanilla ice cream.

Index

Acknowledgements

My biggest thank you goes to my mum, the unsung hero of this book, and to my dad for all his memories of 'Old' Molfetta. Next, my debt of gratitude is to my husband Alessandro for his support during the writing of the book and his undiminishing appetite as he tried each recipe with our children: he is very much looking forward to the follow-up.

A special thank you to my publisher Natalie Bellos and everyone at Bloomsbury for believing in this book, and to my half-Puglian agent Lorella Belli, the first to see the potential in my idea. A huge thank you goes to Hattie Ellis, who has patiently worked on the final draft of this book, suggesting great improvements. Thank you, also, to Christian Müller for his contribution to the early drafts of *Mammissima*.

Heartfelt thanks to Jonathan, the photographer, to Emily and Cynthia, the food and prop stylists, to Georgia, the book designer, to Babeth, the illustrator, and to all the helpers, testers and nutritionists who were involved in this project: without their patient and passionate work, this book would not be half as beautiful or accurate.

A collective thank you to the town of Molfetta and to all my friends there and here in London – in particular Agnese, Anna, Annamaria, Chiara, Claudia, Isabella, Lorena, Nanda, Rita, Sabrina, to mention only a few – as well as my Aunties and the rest of my family. All the others are gratefully acknowledged in my heart.